Anonymous

Westward to the Far East

A guide to the Principal cities of China and Japan with a note on Korea

Anonymous

Westward to the Far East
A guide to the Principal cities of China and Japan with a note on Korea

ISBN/EAN: 9783337191917

Printed in Europe, USA, Canada, Australia, Japan

Cover: Foto ©Andreas Hilbeck / pixelio.de

More available books at **www.hansebooks.com**

WESTWARD

TO

THE FAR EAST

A GUIDE

TO THE PRINCIPAL CITIES OF

CHINA AND JAPAN

WITH

A NOTE ON KOREA.

BY

ELIZA RUHAMAH SCIDMORE.

FOURTH EDITION

ISSUED BY

THE CANADIAN PACIFIC RAILWAY COMPANY,

1893.

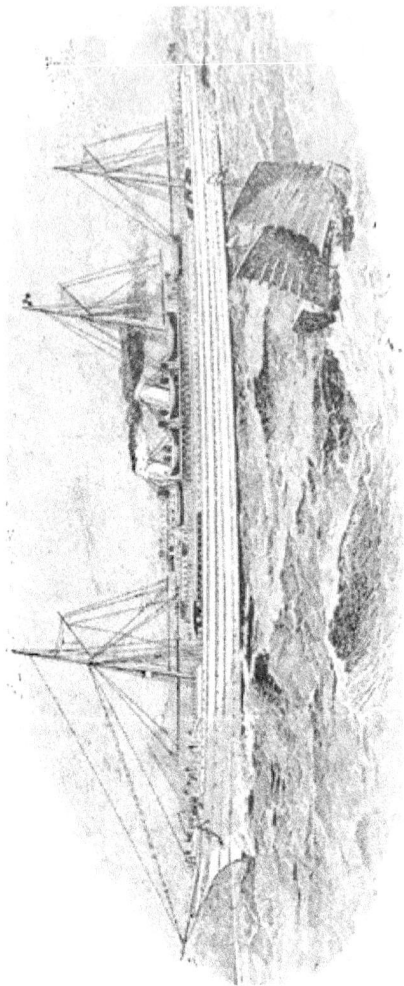

PREFACE.

"Westward to the Far East" is intended to supply general information in a concise form to those who may be desirous of visiting Japan and China, as well as to serve as a guide to those visiting those portions of the Orient by the Canadian Pacific Route. It is not an elaborately descriptive work, nor is it a mere bald statement of times, distances and measurements. It indicates the chief points of beauty and interest along the route and in Japan and China, dealing at sufficient length with each subject to satisfy the casual observer, and referring those who desire more detailed information to the several sources from which that may be obtained. It is intended to tell the possible traveler what there is to be seen and the actual traveler how to see it. It should be, if its author's good intention is fulfilled, interesting to the one and useful to the other. It is the result of personal observation and enquiry prompted by the desire to acquire the knowledge most useful to a tourist, and while being a trustworthy guide to those traveling in the countries referred to, will teach others a great deal about China and Japan which they cannot fail to be interested in knowing.

Those who have made up their minds to take this enjoyable trip will, of course, require information—which being subject to change is not found in the guide book—concerning sailings of steamships, baggage allowances, tickets, connections, etc., for which application should be made to one or other of the Canadian Pacific Railway Company's Agents. And such intending travelers will probably like to have the companion, "The New Highway to the Orient," a handsomely illustrated pamphlet, which tells of the journey across the continent, and which the agents of the company will furnish with pleasure to any one desirous of reading it.

D. McNICOLL,

General Passenger Agent, C. P. R.

MONTREAL, *January*, 1893.

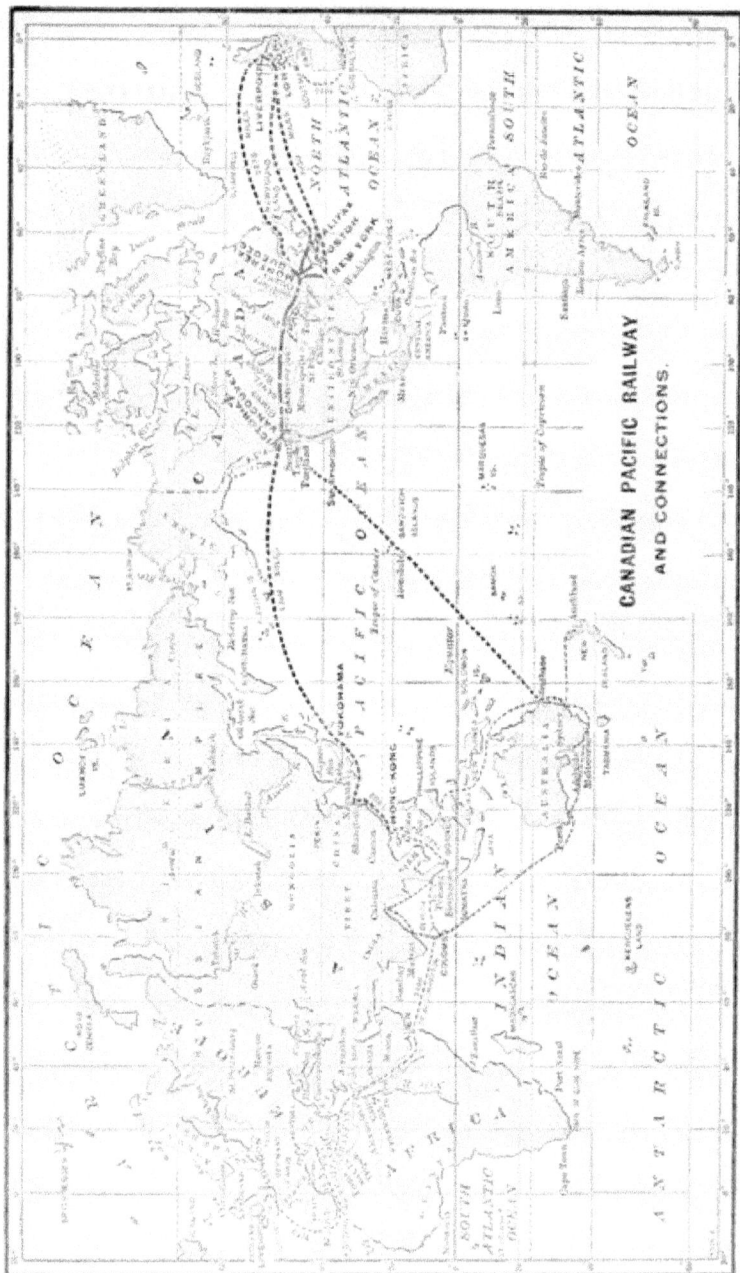

CANADIAN PACIFIC RAILWAY.
AND CONNECTIONS.

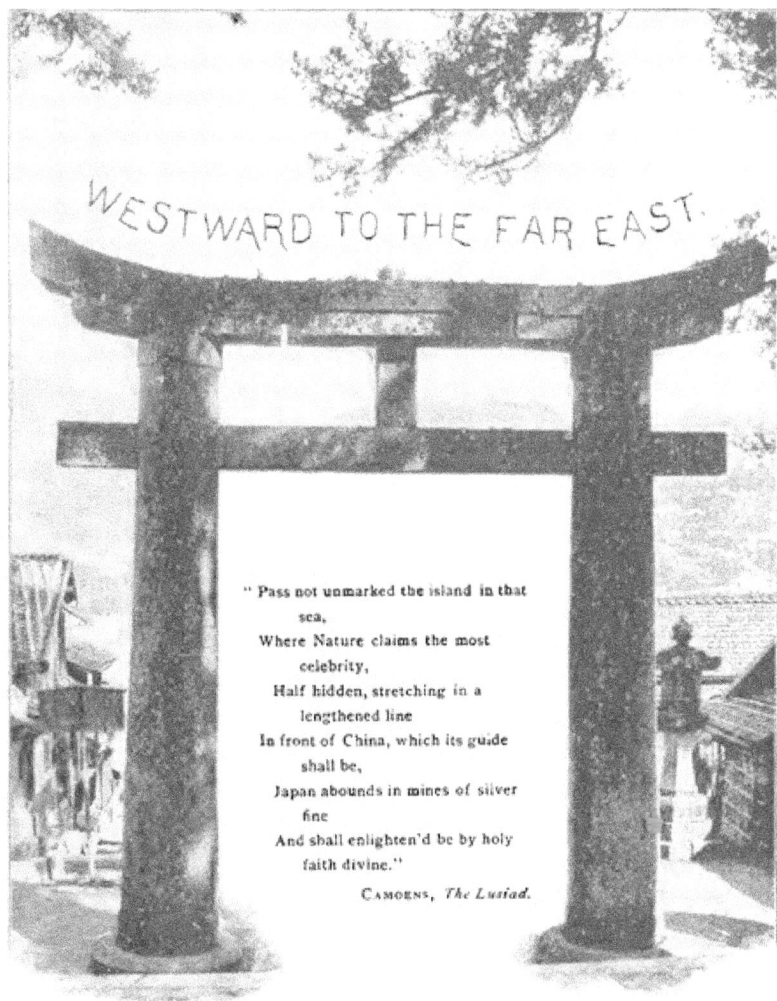

WESTWARD TO THE FAR EAST.

" Pass not unmarked the island in that
    sea,
Where Nature claims the most
    celebrity,
    Half hidden, stretching in a
        lengthened line
In front of China, which its guide
    shall be,
Japan abounds in mines of silver
    fine
And shall enlighten'd be by holy
    faith divine."

CAMOENS, *The Lusiad.*

I.

When Columbus sailed westward to find a shorter route to the
Indies, he was thinking as well of the fabled Zipangu of which Marco
Polo had heard at the court of Khublai Khan. Leaving San Salva-
dor and sighting Cuba, the great admiral was sure that Zipangu's
palace, with its roof, floors and windows " of gold, in plates like slabs
of stone, a good two fingers thick," was near at hand.

Fortunately for us, Japan was held in reserve for this century and this generation, and this exquisite country—different in itself from the rest of the world and all this side of the planet, as quaint and unique, as beautiful and finely finished as one of its own *netsukes* or minute works of art—delights the most jaded traveler and charms every one who visits it.

Columbus failed to find this Zipangu, or Jeh Pun, the Land of the Rising Sun; but Pinto did in 1542, and made possible the work of St. Francis Xavier and the early Jesuit fathers, but for whose interference with political affairs the country would not have been closed to all foreign intercourse until Commodore Perry's visit in 1853. The sperm whale was the innocent factor in this great result, and after quoting Michelet's praise of the whale's service to civilization, Nitobe* says, "that the narrow cleft in the sealed door of Japan, into which Perry drove his wedge of diplomacy, was the rescue of American whalers." From providing a grudging refuge for shipwrecked and castaway mariners, Japan now welcomes visitors from all the world and bids them enjoy an Arcadia where many things are so strange and new that one might as well have journeyed to another planet.

Within a few years pleasure travelers around the world have more than quadrupled in numbers, and a girdling of the earth is now the *grand tour*, which a little round of continental Europe used to be. The trip to Japan for Japan's sake alone is altogether an affair of these later days. "More travelers, better ships; better ships, more travelers," is an old axiom in shipping circles, and there is proof in the increasing number of trans-Pacific passengers and the presence of the Canadian Pacific Railway Company's fleet of Empress steamships which carry them across the greater ocean. With their close connection with the company's transcontinental railway a new era of travel began. There is every inducement and temptation to make the circuit of the globe, and Japan fairly beckons one across and along this highway to the Orient. With but two changes, one may go from Hong Kong to Liverpool, more than half way around the globe; and from Hong Kong to the Atlantic steamer a uniform decimal system of coinage solaces a tourist's existence.

Time and distance have been almost annihilated by modern machinery, and the trip from New York to Yokohama takes no longer now than did the trip from New York to Liverpool but a few years ago. Ten days after leaving Yokohama the *Empress of Japan* had arrived at Vancouver, and in less than fifteen days from leaving Japanese shores its passengers were in New York and Boston. Inside of sixty days one may leave New York, cross the continent and the Pacific, spend four weeks in the cities and famous places of Japan, and return again to New York; where, if he commit himself to Atlantic ships and waves, he will remember and more keenly appreciate the delights of the Pacific voyage.

Each year is Europeanizing and changing Japan, and the sooner

---

* "Intercourse Between the United States and Japan," by Inazo (Ota) Nitobe. Baltimore: John Hopkins. Pren., 1891

the tourist goes the more Japanese will he find those enchanting islands. Every season is a good season to visit Japan, and in every month of the year he will find something peculiar to that season in addition to the usual features. The time of the cherry blossoms and the season of the chrysanthemums are the gala weeks of the year, and during those April and October fêtes the climate leaves little to be desired. The somewhat rainy season of June and September render those months the least desirable, and the heat of midsummer is a little trying to some ; yet from the first poetic days of springtime to the end of the longdrawn autumn the out-door life gives all interest and color which the winter months lack. The autumn usually merges into an Indian summer which may last until January, and the frost summons such a carnival of color at which the Canadian and the American, used to their own brilliant autumnal foliage, may marvel. In midwinter Tokio is crowded, parliament is in session, the court is in full social activity, pageants and holidays are many, and even at its worst the weather is a gentle contrast to that of the continent across the Pacific.

"The Japanese," says Percival Lowell,* makes love to Nature, and it almost seems as if Nature heard his silent prayer and smiled upon him in acceptance ; as if the love-light lent her face the added beauty that it lends the maid's. For nowhere in this world, probably, is she lovelier than in Japan : a climate of long, happy means and short extremes, months of spring and months of autumn, with but a few weeks of winter in between ; a land of flowers, where the lotus and the cherry, the plum and wistaria, grow wantonly side by side ; a land where the bamboo embosoms the maple, where the pine at last has found its palm-tree, and the tropic and the temperate zones forget their separating identity in one long self-obliterating kiss."

II.

A daylight trip up the Hudson and past Lake Champlain, or a night in a sleeping car, puts the transatlantic or the New York traveler at the beginning of his journey. From Montreal to Vancouver the broad highway of the Canadian **ACROSS THE CONTINENT.** Pacific Railway bands the continent and joins the two ocean tides, as if only a broad quay separated them. In luxurious cars, where he dines and sleeps, bathes, smokes and reads as in a hotel, he beholds the panorama of the continent. There is revealed to him every physical feature of the new world, the great lakes, the great rivers, the plains and prairies, forests and swamps, and finally the greatest mountain ranges of the continent succeed one another in the rapidly moving pictures. The engine darts through, climbs over, flanks, encircles and conquers those barriers until, racing down the long cañon with the mad current of the Frazer, it runs out from the level woodland at the head of Burrard's Inlet, and, panting, slows up side by side with the great white steamship that is to convey the

* "The Soul of the Far East " by Percival Lowell. Boston and New York: Houghton, Mifflin & Co., 1888.

traveler across
the ocean, to that
older world where
the human race began.

With his annotated time table—the most excellent and useful piece of railway literature ever devised—the tourist has a key and bird's-eye view of the continent beside him, and with his own pencilings by the way on its blank leaves, it becomes the complete journal and record of his days on the overland train. There is a new object lesson in geology and botany to be studied through car windows each day and much of ethnology as well. For the first day the train races through a half covered glacier garden, and the marks of the great ice sheet that ground down the Laurentian slopes are so plain that one expects some next turn to show a rumpled ice stream pouring through a ravine, rather than another lake encircled by the forest.

On the second day, the glacier garden continues on a larger scale, and on the left the view ranges out over that inland sea, the vast blue Lake Superior. The north shore is the paradise of sportsmen and anglers, and one glimpses lakes, clear white streams and rushing rivers whose names are synonyms for trout—six-pounders, too. At Fort William, the travelers who have chosen the lake route from Owen Sound across Lake Huron and through the picturesque Sault Ste. Marie to Lake Superior, join the train, and at Winnipeg the Chicago and St. Paul contingent are waiting. As the train fills with other trans-Pacific voyagers, each tourist is convinced that all the world is bound for Japan, and that his particular party is but a fraction of some great excursion.

LAKE SUPERIOR.

Winnipeg, the prairie city, distanced all records of booming towns when the railroad reached the Selkirk Settlements on Red River, isolated for a hundred years in the heart of the continent.

WINNIPEG.

A busy western city grew like magic around the old Hudson's Bay Company fort, and instead of exchanging beads and paint with Indian trappers, that mercantile corporation displays the latest fashions in plate glass show windows and maintains a general store for city needs. The main street, with its handsome buildings, its large hotels, electric lights and electric cars, is busy at all times of the year, but most picturesque in midwinter, when every one wears fur garments and sleigh-bells jingle in the dry, electric air.

The French Canadian, the woodsman and the birch bark canoe cease at the prairie's edge. Winnipeg is the central station and half-way house of the continent, and after a two hour's rest one takes a fresh start on the journey with freshened cars. All beyond that point is the far, golden, remote, wide West, full of wonders, picturesqueness, wild life and adventure. The prairies, level as placid seas or rolling like the ocean in its storms, stretch unbroken to the base of the Rockies. The grassy plains, where the buffalo roamed by millions, are now mosaiced with wheat fields, checkered with these squares of intensest green or golden yellow grain or the black of plowed loam, and tall elevators stand by the tracks like lighthouses on the level sea. The only reminders of the herds that used to blacken the prairies are in the melancholy piles of bleached bones beside the track—bones that are gathered all over the buffalo country and sold at two dollars a cord to be shipped to sugar refineries. The noble Blackfeet and Crows crouch on the station platforms at Qu'Appelle, Moosejaw, Swift Current and Medicine Hat selling polished buffalo horns, or polished ox horns, which do as well for the tourist trade, and hiding their heads from amateur photographers until paid to pose. The Northwestern Mounted Police, alert for smugglers and disturbers of the Indian peace, show their gay uniforms at all these prairie stations, and are as favorite subjects for touch-the-button photographers as the retired red warriors, bucks and braves temporarily out of the scalping business.

THE PRAIRIES.

At daylight, a high blue wall bars the west, resolves itself into spurs, peaks and long, overlapping ranges, and shows a more impenetrable front as the train races toward it and ploughs into a cleft at its base. One enters the mountains and leaves the plains behind as abruptly as if he had passed through a door in an artificial wall. The whole world changes. Mountains tower about one, each one rising alone and distinct from the narrow level of the valleys ; each mountain as sharp, free cut and isolated as a pyramid built by human hands. Geology and world-building are written as plainly as printed text, and the processes by which these masses were uplifted are so apparent, that one can fancy the strata still in motion, groaning and creaking as they are forced up and bent almost at a right angle with their old horizontal levels.

THE ROCKIES.

Even the most hurried tourist should save three days of grace for his overland tour, and spend one of them at Banff, just within the mountain wall. The Canadian Government has reserved a National Park twenty-six miles long and ten miles wide, and in its midst, surrounded by the finest peaks, sections of strangely and magnificently tilted strata, the Canadian Pacific Company has provided a perfect hotel. The building is perched on a knoll above the blue Bow River, and commands such views toward every point of the compass that only a revolving room on the roof could give the guest the outlook he most desires. He may rejuvenate himself in the magic hot sulphur waters in a hotel tub, or he may plunge into a natural swimming pool of warm water in a domed cave ; and by horse, foot, wheel and boat he may explore the surrounding Rocky Mountain Park for weeks without exhausting its wonders.

BANFF.

From Banff to Laggan the scenery is most magnificent and the Rockies equal all of one's expectations. Gigantic peaks and battlemented walls enclose the narrow valley, and glaciers and snow fields clothe the upper reaches, beyond and among which lie the so-called Lakes of the Clouds, bits of water framed in mountain walls that rival the best of Swiss and Norwegian scenery. A three-mile wagon road has been cleared through the pine woods from Laggan to Lake Louise, the beginning of cloudland. The railway company has built a log châlet near the lake shore, where the tourist may lunch, and enjoy simple comforts if he wishes to prolong his stay and dwell awhile in the wilderness.

Lake Louise, with its tremendous peaks and precipices, its glaciers and snow fields, its stretch of mirror waters that nearer show **THE LAKES IN** a depth of color unapproached by the other lakes, **THE CLOUDS.** has drawn forth all the adjectives its visitors could command. Yet its loveliness can only be suggested to those who have not climbed among the slender tapering spruces and literally waded among the wild flowers on the high mountain meadows. Mirror Lake, still further up among the clouds, is a pool of different hue, more closely hemmed by mountain walls striped, overspread and finely fretted with snow banks ; and every detail shows double, the clearest and sharpest reflections covering the whole unruffled surface of the lake. There are magnificent views down to the Bow Valley and across to further ranges as one follows these upper trails, picking his way in and out of forests, and across acres of heathery pink and white brianthus and pale green cassiopeia, and beds of blue bells, gentians, cyclamens, anemones, daisies, buttercups, and Indian pinks. The edelweiss is found in the highest flower beds, and footprints of mountain goat and mountain sheep tell what other visitors these flower-gemmed meadows attract.

Lake Agnes is third and last in the trio of lakelets, and in the high, thin air every detail of its further shores are as clearly seen as if near at hand. Waterfalls dropping in slender filaments from the higher snow banks, fill the air with a distant, constant undertone, and the fleecy clouds sail over a second sky lying in the lake, and play hide and seek with the doubled peaks.

The wonders of the Rockies are not nearly exhausted when one takes train again at Laggan. Soon Mt. Stephen looms, first ahead and then directly overhead, as one is tobogganed down the cañon at its base. It takes more than two looks to reach to the top, precipitously as it fronts one, and the mountain plays fantastic tricks with the eye as the train moves away from it—the domed mass suddenly bounding from behind a ridge, rising, swelling and seeming to advance toward one as the engine shrieks and madly races away from it.

Another great mountain range bars the way and the train creeps along shelves and ledges of the cañon of cañons leading to the summit of the Selkirk range. The views backwards, below, across and overhead are more and more magnificent as one catches glimpses between the tunnels. After gaining the ridge, the train races from

Rogers Pass down to Glacier station, where another of the company's hotels invites the tourist to spend his third day of grace, and as many more hours as he can command.

The hotel is 4300 feet above either ocean, and the broad stream of the Selkirk Glacier is seen curling over and pouring down the slope at the end of the great horseshoe valley.

THE GREAT SELKIRK GLACIER. Advancing only one foot a day, the sun matches its might against the ice and keeps the forefoot of the glacier almost stationary at the head of the ravine. One may see the glacier very satisfactorily from the car window and note the pale greens and blues of the crevasses breaking the glimmering surface ; but he who stops may walk a mile and a half through the woods and, mounting the grimy ice cliffs, wander as far as he will over the crackling surface. Asulkan, "the home of the mountain goat," rises behind the hotel, but that nervous beast, as well as his colleague, the big horn sheep, have taken to further pastures since the iron horse invaded their realms and began its incessant shrieking and tooting on the grades of the Illicilliwaet Cañon.

Crossing the youthful Columbia again, the train climbs a third mountain range and by the Eagle pass of the Gold Range reaches the shore of the great Shuswap Lake. The tourist, who has made the journey without stop, has then enjoyed some sixteen hours of the finest mountain scenery on the continent ; is grimed with his day in the observation car, and deafened with the echo of cañons ; and as the Shuswap mountains shade to purple in the late summer sunset, he is too exhausted to agree or disagree with those less weary ones who pronounce the evening hours along the lake the crowning glory of the whole day's ride.

As if this were not enough for a transcontinental trip, there follow the sunrise lights on the painted cliffs, the rose and orange, vermilion and umber walls of the steep cañons of the Thompson River. Last comes the splendid race with the Fraser to the sea, and a final speeding through the Cascade forests, where trees of gigantic size, a tangle of ferns and densest undergrowth tell of a new climate and conditions, the other shore, the Cordilleran slopes of the continent.

At Vancouver a still larger and better hotel has been provided by the same far-seeing company, and although in the heart of the town, its site affords it a fine mountain outlook.

VANCOUVER. Southward shines Mount Baker, a radiant pyramid of eternal snow, whose fascination grows upon one, and which Vancouver folk are beginning to look upon with an affection and reverence that shadow the feeling of the Japanese for their sacred Fujiyama. A mountain wall rises straight across the harbor, and behind it is the lake from which the city receives its water supply, the pipes being laid in the bed of the inlet, whose waters, too, are so clear that one hardly believes them salt. In them float such large and richly-colored jelly-fish and medusæ as one only expects to find in tropic waters, and at low tide the piles of the older wharves offer such an aquarium and museum of marine life as would be worth an admission fee on the Atlantic coast.

Vancouver can pleasantly entertain a waiting voyager for a few days. Its streets combine frontier and sea-faring, backwoods, European, American and Oriental conditions and people. One curio shop sells basket work, silver and slate carvings brought in canoes by the coast Indians, and at the next door all the Orient is set before one by Chinese and Japanese traders who add to their stock by each arriving steamer. A mountain of tea chests is unloaded from each *Empress*, and a mountain of sacked flour and cotton in bales takes their place. In one shop delicate jeweler's scales weigh the miners' gold dust poured from buckskin bag or tin box; in another shop lean, yellow Chinese fingers manipulate the silk strung scales with which the smokers' opium is measured out. A street of trim villas, with beautifully-kept lawns and gardens, becomes a roadway through the forest primeval, and the nine miles of carriage road through Stanley Park show one a forest as dense as a tropical jungle. Where the sombre Douglas spruce grows thickest, there is only a dim, green twilight under their branches at noonday, and the road is a mere tunnel through the original forest. Bushes, vines, ferns and mosses riot there, cedars of California proportions amaze one, and the voyager should even rise before the lark, rather than leave without seeing what a northwest coast forest is like.

Coming out of the forest to the brow of a cliff, which stands as a gateway to the inlet, one may look almost straight down upon the decks of passing steamers, and on the rocks below lies the wreck of the *Beaver*, the first steamer that ever churned Pacific waters. It came round the Horn in 1836, bringing its boiler and engines as freight, and they were put in place in the Columbia River. As a Hudson's Bay Company's steamer, the *Beaver* was known to the Indians from Astoria to Chilkat, and much respected by them as a "King George" ship, while Lieut. Pender made soundings and surveys for his British Columbia coast charts. From that estate it fell, and rather then remain a Victoria tug-boat the *Beaver* committed nautical suicide in 1889 by dashing itself against the cliffs of Stanley Park.

Close past it sail the three great white *Empresses* on each inward and outward trip ; the first and the latest steamships in the Pacific for an instant side by side. Far more than a half century of invention would seem to lie between the crude and primitive little engine that beat within the *Beaver's* sides and the powerful machinery that propels these floating palaces, supreme efforts of Barrow-in-Furness master marine builders.

Nothing that could be devised in those Lancashire yards was omitted to make the three *Empresses* triumphs of such arts. Strength and speed were first considerations, and with their steel hulls, double bottoms, watertight compartments, twin screws, triple expansion engines and straight record of over nineteen knots an hour, the conditions

THE STEAMSHIPS.

13

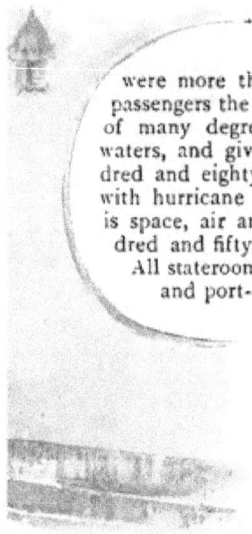

were more than fulfilled. First for the comfort of the passengers the ships were painted white, making a difference of many degrees temperature between decks in southern waters, and giving them a spick and span look. Four hundred and eighty-five feet in length and fifty-one feet beam, with hurricane deck, cabins and staterooms amidships, there is space, air and steadiness to be enjoyed by the one hundred and fifty cabin passengers which each ship can carry. All staterooms have electric lights, and while electric fans and port-hole scoops give air in tropic regions, steam heat cheers and comforts on the northern parallels. Electric fans above the tables replace the flapping flounce of the eastern punkah, and the creaking bar, and the sleepy punkah boy with his string, are no longer known. Chinese servants in caps and rustling blue blouses minister silently with velvet tread, automatic in their perfection, and the steward's crew are drilled to the wants of the clubmen and *gourmets* of the Far East, where dinner is a far more important and serious affair than in England itself. The traveler soon adopts "boy" as the appellation of every kind of servant, his luncheon becomes "tiffin," he claps his hands quite as much as he rings the bell or presses the button, and the yellow servitors appear as quickly and silently as Ram Lal, with his keyhole entrances and cloud exits; and the ease, the luxury, and all the creature comforts of the Far East begin to work their spell before many Pacific meridians are left behind.

III.

While a China steamer lies at Vancouver wharf, the whole town is conscious of the fact. When the "blue peter" flies at the mast head Vancouver keeps an eye on the inlet, and when the ship sails all Vancouver goes down to the wharf and speeds the *Empress* on her way. The ship often waits as late as fifteen o'clock in the afternoon, by the Canadian Pacific's twenty-four hour time system, in order to get the last passengers and the European mails from the overland train; in the short winter days it usually waits till the following morning. Then the lines are cast loose and the ship floats out into the stream. Vancouver cheers and bids the *Empress* adieu; and gathering speed, the ship threads the Narrows, sends a great ripple across the *Beaver's* green bones, gives one a glimpse into that magnificent fiord, Howe Sound, and then courses through the sea of islands, the long, island-studded stretch of the Gulf of Georgia. For four hours the ship winds its way through land-locked waters before it reaches the open ocean and begins the voyage to the Orient, away from the New World to the Old World, out of the West into the East.

THE OCEAN START.

A smoke cloud on the Vancouver Island shore tells of Nanaimo's coal mines, where the ship's bunkers were filled, and always in the east shines Mount Baker, its white cone showing as long as land is in sight. Strange markings on the water tell where the fresh water of the Frazer River, with its different density and temperature, floats above, or cuts through the salt water in a body, showing everywhere a sharply defined line of separation. As silently as if sailing, not a beat of its great engines felt, the ship goes swiftly over almost glassy waters, among numerous islands, until passing between San Juan and Vancouver Islands it sights Beacon Hill, with its many suburban villas, and slows for a few minutes off the outside wharves of Victoria. The pilot clambers down to a waiting boat, carrying last letters and messages ashore and the last passengers are embarked. The city of Victoria is all but hidden far within its rock-rimmed and intricate harbor, and the naval station of Esquimault only declares itself by the mast heads showing beyond the tree-tops.

No one should sail away thinking he has seen all, when he has not visited the one city of Victoria on the Western continent. Other cities named from Her Majesty have each their distinctive charm, but the Victoria of Vancouver is not surpassed. The real harbor upon which

VICTORIA,
B. C.

the city fronts is a broad basin reached by such a narrow passage between tree-covered points that larger steamers do not attempt to enter it, stopping instead at the outside wharf at the extreme eastern end of the city. So intricate is this inside harbor, with its many smaller bays and arms, that no tide table has ever been made out for it, and that mystery of the moon and the sea remains a riddle to scientist and mariner. On one arm of the harbor stands the old Hudson's Bay Company's storehouses, reminders of that day when those earliest pioneers erected their block-houses and traded with the Indians for pelts. Slowly the town grew, Frazer River, Cariboo and Cassiar mining booms bringing prospectors, pioneers and settlers to know the place and slowly add to its importance in that long ago before the railway. While British Columbia was an independent colony and Sir James Douglas and the other governors reigned undisturbed on this remote coast, Victorians had an even greater pride in their city. Those were the good old days of which it is most interesting to hear, but since the province joined with Canada its fortunes have grown apace, and the sentiment of the older residents has given way to great satisfaction with its wonderful later development and prosperity.

A railway connects the city with the coal mines and Nanaimo; a railway bridge spans a narrow arm of the harbor; electric cars whizz up and down the streets, across James Bay to the outside wharf; its hotels have multiplied and grown; its streets and shops make brave, gay showing, its Chinatown beguiles the tourist of many hours and dollars, and the passing traveler leaves with regret, hoping always to return.

Victoria has the perfect climate according to the Princess Louise, who seeing it smothered in the billows of bloom of its early summer could not say enough in its praise. Southern California hardly shows more of beauty in city door-yards than one sees in Vancouver and Victoria, where the rose, the honeysuckle, and the fuchsia in particular, astonish one by their wild luxuriance. A century ago the natural clearings matted with wild roses amazed Marchand, the old French *voyageur*, who compared Vancouver shores to the rose-covered slopes of Bulgaria. Ferns measuring eight and twelve feet in length, from root to tip of a single frond, entangle themselves by the roadside as foreground to the original forest setting, and every drive shows more of wild beauty and wonder. The sportsman and the angler find as much of delight in the surrounding country as the botanist, and every brave Briton feels pride in the splendid ships at Esquimault, the naval station just west of the city. There a dry-dock, ship-yard, foundries and workshops, storehouses and magazine supply the fleet that, cruising from the Dominion to Chili, looks after British interests on this side of the Pacific.

Up the Arm all young Victoria rows and sings on summer nights when sunset lingers so late; and to pull up this long, narrow, winding arm of the sea, through its gorge where the waters swirl and boil, and return with the tide bearing one swiftly back again, is an excursion that delights the Victorian heart.

Life goes easily and delightfully in this city by the western sea. Its citizens are sociable and hospitable. There is much tea and tennis, boating and picnicing, dining and dancing, and military and naval uniforms brighten such scenes and maintain the official flavor of society at this old provincial capital.

Leaving Victoria, the shore scenery grows finer as the ship, heading almost due westward through the Straits of Fuca, the mythical Straits of Anian, follows the sinking sun. The Olympic range stands as a giant sea-wall along the Washington shore, the Angel's Gate, a gap in the range just over the town of Port Angeles, showing a splendid snow peak in far perspective. Vancouver's shores slope from park-like and cultivated tracts by the water to leagues of unbroken wildernesses that clothe the mountain slopes to their very summits. Groups of black canoes drawn up on shore, columns of smoke before bark huts, can be seen with the glasses, and all the water's edges are picturesque. Race Rock Light, a mere candlestick standing on the water, signals the steamer adieu with the Union Jack by day, and flashes its white light by night. Far across, Cape Flattery's light-keeper hails with the stars and stripes, and then, as she follows the dying day, there lies before the *Empress* the limitless western ocean, where the sun sets, the sun rises, and time begins.

This ocean voyage of 4300 miles begins at the 49th parallel of north latitude, and Yokohama lies at 35 degrees 20 minutes north.

THE VOYAGE. By going further north, where the degrees of longitude converge, the distance across is lessened. On the westward course, the *Empresses* curving route runs near enough to the Aleutian chain for one to see the shores of Amchitka Island, if the day be clear, or discern the glow of its volcano reflected in the sky at night. The "wolf's long howl" is not heard by the mariner on his midnight watch, as despite the poet, the animal does not inhabit Unalaska nor any of the island chain. Instead, blue foxes are raised for their pelts, and Atka in especial is all one blue fox ranch or peltry preserve. There are no settlements on these islands and but scant supplies of food and fuel for the wretched Aleutians living in half underground habitations. When the passes between these islands are surveyed and charted the course to Japan can be shortened by curving through them and along the higher parallels in Behring Sea; and the future trans-Pacific cable will have a land station on one of the Aleutians, and following their line, cross to the Kuriles or the Kamschatkan peninsula and join the Siberian telegraph lines.

Crossing the line is the great incident of a Pacific voyage, and the 180th meridian that marks the division between the Eastern and the Western hemispheres, and is the exact **A DAY LOST**. antipode of Greenwich, is almost midway in the course. In going out to Japan a day is dropped from the calendar, and in going eastward the day is doubled. One goes to bed on Monday night and wakens on Wednesday morning, or, on the return trip, he arises to live over again and repeat the incidents of the day before. On account of ship's discipline, certain privileges and routine duties of the crew belonging to Sunday, that day is seldom dropped or doubled, and if the meridian is passed on Sunday notice is rarely paid it. Convivial passengers celebrate the crossing of the line, and the exact moment of transit is always known. The imaginative are bidden to feel the grating of the ship's keel over the meridian, and to see the line itself through a marine glass that has a cobweb thread across one lens. The up hill of the voyage is over, and the descent down hill from the great meridian, out of the West and into the East, is begun.

When the ship gets as far west at 160 degrees east from Greenwich the warmer and moister air of the Japan Stream is felt, and if it be in the summer months, the traveler will be glad to have some lighter clothing at hand. Otherwise he needs the same warm and serviceable clothing in the North Pacific as in the North Atlantic.

Life on one of the Canadian Pacific steamships presents many attractions that do not appear on the Atlantic liner. The passenger need not live below the water line, nor at either end of a see-saw to begin with, and sea-sickness is not **LIFE AT SEA**. the condition of so large a proportion of his fellows. Either the tourist is a better sailor by the time he reaches Balboa's presumably placid ocean, or else he gets his sea legs sooner on its longer swells. The best part of the deck space is not taken up with

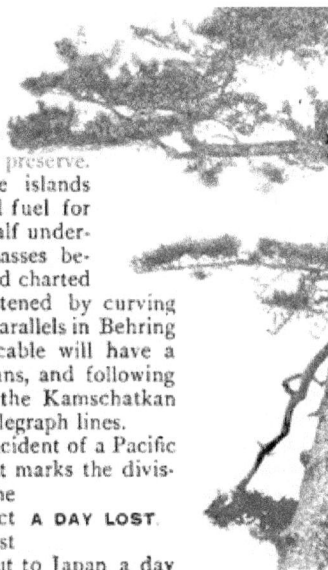

rows of mummies, laid out in steamer chairs, and the fetching and
carrying of broths and doses are not the usual and nauseous incidents
of deck life.   So many nationalities are represented, such cosmo-
politans and veteran travelers are gathered together on one of these
Pacific steamers, that the complacent young tourist, whose town and
family viewed him as a Columbus or a Stanley, when he started to
circle the globe, shrinks into nothingness beside the tea, silk, or opium
merchant at his elbow, who is making his twentieth or thirtieth round
A Manilla or Java planter, a teakwood or pearl merchant from Siam,
the liverless Anglo-Indian, the serious Briton in Chinese service, and
the commercial traveler, who firmly believes that "Asia's my spot,"
whether it be Col. Sellers's eye-water or a newer commodity he aims
to introduce to those millions of customers—all these and many
missionaries, as well, meet on board, and constitute the inhabitants
of the ship's small world.   Veteran travelers, "the oldsters" of the
East, have their regular whist set, long-running tourneys enliven the
smoking room, games on the broad decks divert the company, and
everything is done for the entertainment of the travelers.   If a ball
is wanted, the promenade deck is enclosed with flags, a few more
electric lights are connected, a piano is brought up, and lo! a ball
room worthy of Pacific dancers.

   No sail is sighted between the two shores; no icebergs ever float
in the North Pacific; and a whale, a seal, a school of flying fish or
Portuguese men-of-war, or a night of phosphorescent waves are the
memorable incidents.   Great as the wave scenery may sometimes be
up by 50 and 51 degrees, the Pacific is a much more reliable and
steady-going ocean than "the mournful and misty Atlantic," and the
typhoon is its only dreaded storm.   Generated in the China Sea,
the *tai fun* (great wind) often circles out into the greater ocean before
it expends itself.   The barometer always gives long warning, and
many people are so sensitive to its atmospheric conditions that their
nerves foretell a typhoon almost before the glass begins to fall.

   The typhoon is now so well understood that experienced navi-
gators can tell its direction, when the ship is on its outer circles, at
the centre or beyond its limits, and with a staunch ship in the open
ocean there is nothing to dread but the shaking up and the somewhat
closer air below.   By a rhyming verse the typhoon's seasons are
kept in mind :

> June, too soon.
> July, stand by.
> August, you must.
> September, remember.
> October, all over.

   The Chinese passengers are sometimes interesting.   After filling
the air with paper joss money to propitiate the evil spirits of the
ocean, they seldom come to the top again during the voyage, living
sociably together in the Chinese steerage, where far too much opium
smoking and chatter goes on.   The bones of those who have died
in America are often part of the westbound cargo, and it is con-
tracted that if one of them dies on shipboard he shall not be buried
at sea, but embalmed and carried on to China.

In the leisure days on board, the traveler may devote himself to the literature of Japan, which is extensive. He must read "*The Mikado's Empire*," * which the Japanese themselves acknowledge as the best and most reliable work upon their traditions, history, manners and customs,† until he knows the outlines of the empire's history. He must know of the Sun Goddess, who peopled the islands ; and of Jingo Kogo, the first empress. He must follow the decay of the emperor's power and the usurpation of his functions by the Shogun, until that military vassal became the actual ruler and remained so until the restoration of the emperor to actual power in 1868. He must know of Hideyoshi, the Taiko, the great general of the Middle Ages ; and of Iyeyasu, the Augustus of the Golden Age ; and of Keiki, the last of the Tokugawa Shoguns.

He must learn of the astonishing political changes of this quarter of a century since the Restoration, that marvel of the century —the quick exchange of a feudal **THE JAPANESE** system for a constitutional mon- **RENAISSANCE.** archy ; the extinction of a privileged military class, and the election of a lower house of parliament directly by the people. Theorists are the more puzzled when they confront the race and study the problem on its own ground. "During the last half dozen years," says Mr. E. H. House,‡ "Japan has made more history for itself than in the preceding two and a half centuries of its own annals. It has exhibited transformations the like of which have required ages to accomplish in any other land." One must study Shinto's shadowy forms, a conventional worship of past heroes and abstract qualities, where myths take the place of creed and articles, but which, by imperial command, has been revived as the state religion with the sovereign as its actual head. Buddhism, having come from India by way of China and Korea, is greatly corrupted, and Sinnett is not a guide to its twelve sects.

Of Japanese art, its industrial arts and architecture, Prof. Rein, Dr. Dresser, Prof. Morse, Dr. Anderson, M. B. Huish and Bing have written § in recent years, and the Boston Museum of Fine Arts which displays more and better examples of Japanese art than the tourist will see in Japan itself, is issuing catalogues of its treasures that will become standard text books. In Mr. Conder's treatise on "The

*"The Mikado's Empire," by W. E. Griffis. New York : Harper & Brothers. †See Nitobe, page 145. ‡Harper's Magazine, vol. 46, page 858. § For full titles of books of reference, see list, page 72.

Flowers of Japan and the Art of Floral Arrangement," parts of which Sir Edwin Arnold incorporated in his "*Japonica*," and in Conder's forthcoming volume on landscape gardening, arts new to the rest of the world and refinements western barbarians never dreamed of, are evidenced by the researches of that careful student. The illuminated work on "Japanese Architecture," by Messrs. Gardiner and Conder, now in press, will be also the standard in its line. Of legend and romance Mitford's "Tales of Old Japan" is a treasure house, and Chamberlain's translations and Griffis's "Fairy World" give the tales and folk lore which are keys to half the designs one meets on porcelains, lacquer, bronze and silk. The guide book for his wanderings, the new "Murray's Japan," is the work of that eminent scholar, Basil Hall Chamberlain, and Prof. W. G. Mason. Prof. Chamberlain's "Things Japanese" is a book of general reference, arranged as an encyclopædia, and is as much a necessity for those who would know what they are seeing as the "Murray." Of travels and impressions there are the records of Sir Edward Reed, Miss Bird, Black, Dixon, Lowell and others; and Sir Edwin Arnold, Pierre Loti and Miss Alice Bacon have drawn Japanese women from as many points of view. Everywhere he finds testimony that there are no other people so refined, so courteous, gentle, amiable, interesting and innately æsthetic as these Latins of the Orient.

AMONG THE THOUSAND PINE-CLAD ISLANDS, MATSUSHIMA.

IV.

Often the *Empress* sights land at noon and until dark runs along close to the green Japanese shores. They often approach near enough to Kinkwazan, the sacred island in the Bay of Sendai, for one to see the temples among the trees and the flag flying from the little lighthouse at the island's edge. This Bay of Sendai with Kinkwazan (golden flower mountain) and the thousand pine-clad islands of Matsushima constitute one of the *San-Kei*, the three most beautiful scenes in Japan. Tame deer roam among the temple groves and, in good old Buddhist days, no woman could look upon, much less set her defiling foot upon the sacred isle. Sailors and fishermen pray at the shrines of Kinkwazan, and at the tiny shrine at the summit implore the God of the Sea, who colors the waves to a wondrously pure pale green, to ultramarine, purple and such iridescent hues as one sees nowhere else, save off the golden isle. This Bay of Sendai is rather off the tourist's usual land route, and of the other two most famous scenic resorts in Japan, Ama-no-hashidate is still further off the route on the west coast, and Miajmia, the sacred isle of the Inland Sea, is not seen from the mail steamer's route.

Letting Kinkwazan fade away in the twilight, the *Empress* sights Fujiyama at daybreak, and as the sun springs from its ocean nest and gilds the seaward slopes, the ship rounds Cape King, passes Sagami and Kanonsaki lighthouses on **FUJIYAMA.** the left, and the bugle call announcing the arrival in port often disturbs the breakfast table. In her "Flying Trip Around the World" Miss Bisland says: "A delicate gray cloud grows up along the edge of the water, and slowly a vast conelike cumulus, a lofty, rosy cloud takes shape and form, gathers clearness of outline, deepens

its hue of pink and pearl, melts softly into the gray beneath, soars sharply into the blue above, and reveals Fujiyama, the divine mountain ' * * * A mountain of pink pearl rose out of the sea; and when the gray clouds about its base resolved themselves into land we found that they were the green hills of fairyland. * * * We rose up and perceived that we had come to Fan Land—to the Islands of Porcelain—to Shikishima, the country of chrysanthemums. The place across whose sky the storks always fly by day, and the ravens by night —where cherry blossoms, pink and white, grow out of nothing at all to decorate the foreground, and where ladies wear their eyes looped up in the corners, and gowns in which it is so impossible that any

two-legged female should walk, that they pass their
lives smiling and motionless on screens and jars."

When Fujiyama's pearly cone has grown from a pin point's size
to a majestic peak, and the steamer coursing up the picturesque
Yeddo Bay has made fast at the company's buoy
YOKOHAMA. in Yokohama harbor, Japan encircles one. Steam
launches bear down upon the arriving ship and carry
passengers and mails ashore. Sampans crowd about the steerage
gangway, and the native boatmen and their queer, clean craft are
seen in all their picturesqueness. "It is like the picture books,"
wrote John La Farge in his "Artist Letters."* "The sea was
smooth like the brilliant blank paper of the prints; a vast surface
of water reflecting the light of the sky as if it were thicker
air. Far off streaks of blue light, like finest washes of the brush,
determined distances. Beyond, in a white haze, the square,
white sails spotted the white horizon and floated above it.
* * * Hills of foggy green
marked the near land; nearer us,
junks of the shapes you know, in
violet transparency of shadow, and
five or six war ships and steamers, red and black or white, looking barbarous and out of place, but still as if they were part of us;
and spread all around us a fleet
of small boats, manned by
rowers standing in robes flapping about them, or tucked in
above their waists. There were
so many that the crowd looked blue and white—the color of their
dresses repeating the sky in prose. Still, the larger part were mostly
naked, and their legs and arms and backs made a great novelty
to our eyes, accustomed to nothing but our ship and the enormous
space, empty of life, which had surrounded us for days. The
muscles of the boatmen stood out sharply on their small frames.
They had almost all—at least those who were young—fine wrists
and delicate hands, and a handsome setting of the neck. The foot
looked broad, with toes very square. They were excitedly waiting
to help in the coaling and un-
loading, and soon we saw them
begin to work, carrying great
loads with much good-humored
chattering. Around us played
the smallest boats, with rowers standing up and sculling. Then
the market-boat came rushing to us, its standing rowers bending
and rising, their thighs rounding and insteps sharpening what small
garments they had fluttering like scarfs, so that our fair missionaries
turned their backs to the sight. * * * But the human beings
are not the novelty, not even the Japanese; what is absorbingly
new is the light, its whiteness, its silvery milkiness. We have
come into it as through an open door after fourteen days of the

* Century Magazine, 1890.

Pacific. * * * I have been asking myself whether it would be possible to have sensations as novel, of feeling as perfectly fresh and new, things I knew almost all about beforehand, had we come in any other way or arrived from any other quarter. As it is, all this Japan is sudden. We have last been living at home, are shut up in a ship is if boxed in with our own civilization, and then suddenly, with no transition, we are landed in another. And under what splendor of light, in what contrasting atmosphere! It is as if the sky, in its variations, was the great subject of the drama we are looking at, or at least its great chorus. The beauty of the light and of the air is what I should like to describe, but it is almost like trying to account for one's own mood—like describing the key in which one plays."

The customs examination at the English Hatoba, or landing place, is almost nominal, and only the possession of the strictly contraband drug, opium, can cause trouble. Owing to the existing treaties, accepted by the Japanese when they had not foreseen or understood what foreign trade entailed, five per cent. is the extreme duty that can be levied on foreign goods in any event. Photographic cameras are dutiable, and the snap-shot tourist often repents having made himself so conspicuous in catching his very first impressions on film. Incidentally it may be remarked that the great moisture of the atmosphere hinders the success of instantaneous photographs, and kodaks need to be slowed down to secure even dubious negatives of moving figures. Time exposures are alone to be relied upon in Japan.

With a rush a dozen jinrikishas come forward, and the coolies drop the shafts in a circle around one and invite **JINRIKISHAS.** to the comfortably cushioned seat of the overgrown perambulator. One's sensations upon first riding in one of these vehicles are peculiar, and few can preserve a serious countenance or conceal his self-consciousness while being trundled down the Bund by an absurd little man in tights and a mushroom hat. An eminent divine declared that he wanted to crow and gurgle and shake his hand in a second childhood when he was first taken out in such a baby carriage. The jinrikisha only needs pneumatic tires to furnish the poetry of locomotion

and be the ideal vehicle of the world. The jinrikisha, or kuruma, as it is called in the most polite Japanese speech, was invented or adapted by one Goble, a marine on Commodore Perry's flagship, when he had afterwards returned to Japan as a missionary. Its use dates from 1867 or 1871, as different Japanese authorities assert, but it has quickly spread to China, the Straits, and even to India.

A tariff of jinrikisha and sampan fares will be found on a conspicuous board at the landing place. The fare is ten cents to the hotel or railway station, ten cents by the hour, or seventy-five cents by the day. In going up the hill to the bluff the coolie calls an *atoshi*, or pusher, to help him up the slope, and the passenger pays four cents to this assistant at the top.

All the houses and places of business in Yokohama are known to the coolies by their numbers, which in Japanese and Arabic numerals are fastened to each door or gate. One **HOTELS.** may learn the numerals and their written characters from the hotel menu cards, as each dish is numbered in Japanese at one side of the card and in English at the other side. The guest points to the number and the waiter brings the desired dish.

BILL OF FARE.

Ichi—	1. Porridge.	一
Ni—	2. Fried Fish.	二
San—	3. Boiled Eggs.	三
Shi—	4. Bacon and Eggs.	四
Go—	5. Ham and Eggs.	五
Roku—	6. Poached Eggs.	六
Sh'chi—	7. Omelets.	七
Hachi—	8. Beefsteak.	八
Ku—	9. Cold Roast Beef.	九
Jiu—	10. Cold Corned Round Beef.	十
Jiu ichi—	11. Cold Tongue.	一十
Jiu ni—	12. Fruit.	二十

Ban, meaning "number," is added to each, as *ichi ban*, number one; *go ban*, number five; and *ni jiu ban*, number twenty.

The Grand Hotel (No. 20, or *ni jiu ban*), the Club Hotel (No. 5, or *go ban*), several small hotels in the settlement, and one or two private boarding-places on the Bluff, will receive the stranger. The two larger hotels face on the Bund, or sea-wall, and are as well ordered and kept as hotels of their class in European cities. English or American landlords and French cooks secure every comfort, and electric lights, steam heat, and

band concerts on summer nights, are other features. The Club Hotel maintains a branch house in Tokio, in the buildings long used as the United States Legation. Both hotels are kept on the American plan, rates ranging from three to four dollars per day.

The Yokohama United Club (No. 5) and the German Club (No. 235) are the active centres of the social life of the foreign residents, who number 3700; but this official census includes 2471 Chinese, as well as 616 British, 187 American, **CLUBS.** 170 German and 101 French citizens dwelling in Yokohama. The Yokohama Rowing and Athletic Club has a house on the Bund, adjoining the French Hatoba, with gymnasium, dressing rooms, boat-house and bathing barge. The Cricket and Athletic Club manages the Cricket Grounds in the settlement; the Ladies' Tennis Club cares for the Courts in the Public Gardens on the Bluff; and the Nippon Race Club has its meets each spring and autumn at the Race Course on the Bluff. At the three clubs first named, visitors may be put up by club members, as at a club in a European city, and the usual club comforts and surroundings are found.

The Hong Kong and Shanghai Banking Corporation, on Water Street (No. 2, *ni ban*); the New Oriental Bank Corporation, Limited (No. 11, *jiu ichi ban*); the Chartered Bank of India, Australia and Japan (No. 78, *sh'chi jiu hachi ban*); **BANKS.** the Comptoir d'Escompte de Paris (No. 2, *ni ban*); and the Yokohama Specie Bank (*Shokin Ginko*), a Japanese corporation, all do general banking business. These banks observe the usual national holidays, and are virtually closed during race weeks, which the traveler needs to keep in mind.

Money changers on Main Street and Benten Dori will, for a trifling percentage, change bank notes into the fractional coins so necessary in this land of many small payments.

The Japanese *yen*, at par, corresponds to the American dollar, and is made up of one hundred *sens* which are further divided into ten *rins* each. The depreciated paper *yen* has for **JAPANESE** many years been at an average equal exchange with **MONEY.** the Mexican silver dollar (value about seventy-five cents gold), which is the current coin and monetary unit throughout China and the Far East. From Hong Kong to Montreal one talks of and deals in dollars and cents, realizing handsome premiums in the exchange of Canadian or United States dollars for *yens* or Mexicans.

At the offices of the Canadian Pacific Company's agents, Messrs. Frazar & Co. (No. 200, *ni hiaku ban*), near the Cricket Grounds, and at the branch office on the Bund, passage may be secured and all information given as to future sailings and accommodations, and assistance rendered in arranging for side trips and connections at the different ports of call. The Nippon Yusen Kaisha (United Japanese Company), owned and managed by the government, has a large fleet of coasting steamers, connecting with all the ports of Japan, Korea and North China; and ships are despatched to Vladivostock in Siberia, and Manilla in the Philippine Islands. The Peninsular

and Oriental, the Norddeutscher Lloyd, and the Messageries Maritime Steamship Companies have also offices at Yokohama.

Railways now connect all the principal cities in Japan, and the government has in operation **JAPAN RAILWAYS.** 1048 miles of road, and 483 miles in course of construction. The first lines were built, equipped and managed by English engineers, but all the railway employes are now Japanese.

The post-office is on Main Street and mails depart weekly for Europe, and at an average of ten days interval for America. Japan is a member of the Postal Union, and the uniform five *sen* rate for a foreign letter of fifteen grammes is charged. To any part of Japan the letter postage is two *sen* for each quarter ounce.

The telegraph office is on Main Street (*Denshin Kioku*). There are lines to all parts of Japan, and the charge is fifteen *sen* for the first ten *kana* (square) characters, and ten *sen* for each succeeding ten characters. In a foreign language the charge is five *sen* for each word. A guide, or the hotel clerk, will quickly translate a message into Japanese. There are three cable routes to Europe, the tolls averaging from two to three dollars for each word to New York or Montreal.

Tokio time is kept throughout the empire and is nine hours and twenty minutes in advance of Greenwich time.

When it is twelve o'clock noon, Monday, in Yokohama, it is—

10.47 a.m., Monday,	at Shanghai.		2.48 a.m., Monday,	at Paris.
10.18 " "	at Hong Kong.		2.40 " "	at London.
9.32 " "	at Singapore.		9.40 p.m., Sunday,	at New York.
8.00 " "	at Colombo.		9.40 " "	at Montreal.
8.00 " "	at Calcutta.		8.40 " "	at Chicago.
7.30 " "	at Bombay.		6.40 " "	at San Francisco.
4.48 " "	at Suez.		6.40 " "	at Vancouver.
3.44 " "	at Vienna.			

The British and Russian Consulates and the United States Consulate-General are in line on Nippon Odori, the broad street running westward from the main entrance of the Custom House, **CONSULATES AND PASSPORTS.** which adjoins the English Hatoba. The flagstaffs and the colors of those countries will easily guide one from any point. The Kencho, or office of the local governor, is directly opposite the British Consulate, and the post-office is diagonally across from the United States Consulate-General.

Yokohama Kencho will issue passports for Miyanoshita and vicinity upon application through any Consulate at Yokohama.

Tokio may be visited without a passport, but treaty regulations do not permit any foreigner to go twenty-five miles outside the treaty ports without a passport issued by the Foreign Office of Tokio and stamped by the legation of the applicant. The name of each place which the traveler wishes to visit must be written in the passport. Without such a permit he cannot even buy a railroad ticket to any interior point, and it is quite useless to attempt to evade the restrictions, as no inn-keeper will receive him without a passport, and the hastily-summoned policeman will return the transgressor to treaty limits and future permits will be denied him. Within a few years passport privileges have been much curtailed, and their use is limited to a shorter time.

Applications for passports may be made through the Yokohama Consulates, and two, or at the most three, days usually suffice for the exchange of formalities between them and the Foreign Office at Tokio. By applying in the first morning hours, and paying for a special messenger to Tokio, a passport may be secured the same day. No applications for passports will be considered at the British Consul-ate until the applicant has arrived in Japan. The Canadian Pacific Company's agents may send applications for their passengers' pass-ports to the United States Consulate in advance of a steamer's arrival, and have such permits ready for immediate deliv-ery. The agents must guarantee that such applicants are actual citizens of the United States, and that names and surnames are absolutely correct. Naming Nikko, Chiuzenji, Yumoto, Ikao, Atami, Miyanoshita, Go-temba, Subashiri, Nagoya, Kioto and Nara, he covers all the usual routes of tourist travel, and may take whichever trip offers first. Upon the expiration of the passport it may be renewed; and, in every case, it must be returned to the legation issuing it when it has expired, or when the holder has concluded its use. It is hardly necessary to say that a passport is not transferable, and that some risk attends any such attempt to evade the regulations.

At Kobe any consul will obtain a passport for Kioto from the Kencho, and if the traveler wishes to run up to Kioto for the day that the steamer waits in port, he had best write ahead (inclosing the twenty *sen* fee), and have the permit left for him at one of the Kobe hotels.

Foreign servants must be provided with passports as much as their masters, and most particularly if the serv-ant be Chinese. As a rule the foreign or European servant is quite useless in the Far East. The tourist can easily find a well-trained Japanese "boy" or valet, and an *amah* or lady's maid, who can speak enough English to be of assistance in traveling and add much to one's stay. Their wages range from eight to fourteen dollars, and the

JAPANESE SERVANTS AND GUIDES.

employer does not provide food or lodging in Yokohama or in the larger towns where he makes any stay. In moving about from place to place the servant must of course be provided for. In China he may engage a Chinese boy and carry him as far as Hong Kong, and in the same way secure an Indian servant who will smooth the way across that country.

At either hotel in Yokohama he will find a bulletin board with the cards of the professional guides who are disengaged. A guide is necessary to any one who would comfortably travel in the interior, or off the beaten track, and is an advantage to any one not speaking Japanese. Their guild, the Kaiyusha, authorizes a regular tariff of charges, ranging from one dollar a day upward, according to the number of tourists in the party. The guide's traveling and living expenses are paid by his employer, who saves time and endless annoyance, and misses nothing of interest while in the charge of one of these experienced mentors. The guides of course receive large commissions from merchants and landlords, and it is useless for his employer to attempt to prevent these "squeezes." The oldest foreign residents have never succeeded in worsting the guilds, nor in defying the customs of the Far East. The tourist is warned of the "boy" who speaks a little English, and assumes to guide at a greatly reduced price.

The traveler has little to fear for his health in Japan, where sanitary regulations and quarantine are strictly enforced. There are excellent foreign physicians in each port, foreign **HEALTH AND DOCTORS.** and native hospitals, and well-equipped pharmacies. The foreigner should be careful in diet; drink no water that has not been boiled and filtered, or condensed; avoid shell fish, all ground fruits and uncooked vegetables and iced drinks. In addition, foreign residents throughout Asia at all times wear the cholera belt, a closely-fitted piece of flannel covering the stomach and preventing a sudden chill in that vital region, the fatal symptom in other diseases than cholera. Moreover, he avoids the midday sun, and as a preventive of malaria drinks a cup of hot tea or coffee before descending to the ground floor of a house, or taking the morning bath. In country teahouses and wayside places he can find the counterfeit label of every foreign beverage, but such are wisely avoided. Bottled mineral waters are safest, and that of the Hirano spring near Kobe is very like Apollinaris. Tea in tiny cups is offered everywhere, and satisfies thirst best, but as this fresh and unadulterated green tea is much stronger than the tourist is used to at home, he will find it a powerful stimulant. Shaved ice may always be had for it in summer time. Insect

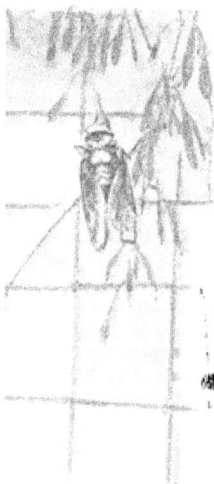

28

powder is a necessary every traveler should carry with him in warm weather, and oil of pennyroyal will help him to lead a charmed life in the oldest tea-houses if he literally anoints himself with it.

V.

The excellent hotels and the foreign life and interests of Yokohama tempt the tourist to linger there; but it is wiser to accomplish his country trips first, and deliver himself over to the seaport's silk and curio shops, photographers, tailors, **KEEPING HOUSE.** tattooers and social life later. If he wishes to make a prolonged stay, he may lease a furnished house all the way from $45 or $50 per month for a small bungalow, up to $300 per month for a more pretentious establishment. Or, taking an empty house, furniture, bedding and table equipments may be rented from the furniture emporiums. Well-trained servants are easily secured, the markets are abundant and absurdly cheap, and nowhere does the householder have such ease and so little care as in one of the foreign settlements of the Far East. Laundrymen charge $2.50 and $3.00 per hundred pieces. A pony trap may be rented for $30 per month, and a saddle horse with *betto*, or running footman, for less. Tailors, both Chinese and Japanese, are many, and their goods cheap; and all through Japan, China and India, where one requires a large supply of thin summer clothing, he can be outfitted quickly, at less cost and more satisfactorily than in Europe or America.

After leaving America, luggage and hand-luggage especially, is no trouble. The luxurious foreign residents in the East travel with mountains of impedimenta. There are always servants and coolies to carry it, and the native measures **LUGGAGE.** his respect by the visible possessions of the tourist. In jinrikisha and mountain trips in Japan, luggage is, of course, reduced to a minimum. The railroads allow sixty pounds of luggage to each ticket.

Besides wandering through the streets of open-fronted shops, watching the mercantile and domestic dramas enacted there, and enjoying the succession of living Japanese tableaux, shopping is the chief amusement of the tourist in **JAPANESE CURIOS.** Yokohama. Curios abound, and art treasures from all parts of the empire come to this largest market. The stranger need not expect to find great treasures in the traditional dingy shop and side street in this modern day of keen appreciation and trade rivalry. But, unless he has had a bent that way and searched great museums and private collections at home, the tourist very often gets his first introduction to Japan's real art products after landing. He finds that the so-called Japanese wares that overflow the bazaars and fancy goods shops in foreign countries are abominations concocted solely for the supposed tastes of outer barbarians, and not used by Japanese at all. Collectors in all other parts of the world long ago drained the country of the choice products of the old artists, but imitations of the old wares and forgeries of the old masters are abundant. In the absence of any public art museums, the tourist has no standards at hand for comparisons, and the curio dealers palm off their spurious treasures the more easily. Connoisseurs are victimized as often as novices, so clever are the imitations, and Makuza Kozan, the great potter near Yokohama, has made imitations of Chinese peach blows and hawthorns which deceived Chinese experts. Since the western world has become so enthusiastic over Japanese paintings, forgeries of Hokusai, Okio and Sosen have been the profitable employment of clever kakemono painters. As original kakemonos by those artists command as much as one thousand *yen*, bargains may be distrusted. The days of bargaining in oriental fashion, of haggling for hours over a few *yens* are fast ending too, and fixed prices and goods marked in plain figures are the rule at the best establishments. The large curio dealers in Yokohama make gorgeous displays in plate glass show windows, invite all to visit their establishments, and if the tourist betrays any interest in curios he will find himself the object of pleasant attentions from rival firms. There are many small curio, or more purely second-hand, shops on Honcho Dori and Benten Dori, on Isezakicho and the Camp Hill road leading to the Bluff, and peddlers soon learn the way to one's apartment.

Isezakicho, a street of museums, side-shows, tents, booths, restaurants, toy-shops and labyrinthine bazaars, will amuse the tourist for several evenings with its street scenes and indoor **AMUSEMENTS** spectacles. With an interpreter, the Japanese theatre will prove a delight and a revelation, and a guide will arrange for a dinner in Japanese style at a tea-house or an eel-house.

From the temple grounds on Nogeyama, the hill at the left of the railway station, a bird's-eye view of the city and harbor may be obtained, with the fort on the Kanagawa cliffs overlooking them. A carriage, or jinrikisha, ride around the Bluff, where are the homes of the foreign residents, past the race-course, and around by the shores of Mississippi Bay, will show one much of beauty and interest in the couple of hours devoted to it. There is good bathing at the Honmoku Beach below Yokohama Bluff, and the tea-house there provides every accommodation for bathers.

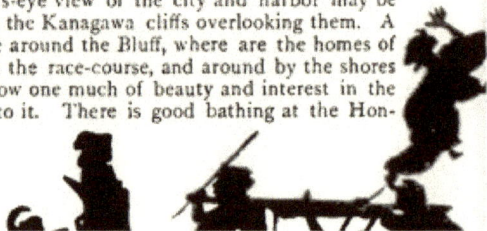

VI.

The *ri* and the *cho* are the Japanese measures of distance. The *ri* is equal to about two and a half English miles, and it takes 36 *chos* to make one *ri*. Fifteen *chos* are a little more than one mile. One *ri* equals 3.9273 kilometres, and it is believed that that decimal system will soon be adopted. On country roads jinrikisha fares are regulated by distance, from eight to fifteen *sen* a *ri* being charged, according to the character of the road, but on all the usual routes, to and from country stations, the exact tariff is known.

No passport is required to visit Kamakura and Enoshima, twenty miles below Yokohama. The railway train will take one to Kamakura (fare 45 *sen* 1st class; 30 *sen* 2d class), landing him near the Temple of Hachiman, an historic shrine where many famous relics are displayed. He may tiffin at the Kaihin-in, a hotel in a pine grove near the beach famous for its cuisine, and a popular resort for foreigners at all seasons.

The colossal bronze statue of Buddha—the Dai Butsu—is a mile distant from the Kaihin-in. The image is fifty feet in height, and after inspecting the temple in its interior, the visitor may be photographed, seated in the lap or on the thumb of Buddha. The priest will mail the **THE DAI BUTSU.** prints to any address given. At the Kotoku-in monastery the behavior of uncivilized tourists forced the priests to post this appeal:

"Stranger, whosoever thou art and whatsoever be thy creed, when thou enterest this Sanctuary remember thou treadest upon ground hallowed by the worship of ages.

"This is the temple of Buddha and the gate of the eternal, and should therefore be entered with reverence."

Driving five miles down the beach the island of Enoshima is reached. At low tide the jinrikisha can go to the foot of one of the steep streets, but at high tide a ferry boat plies across a stretch of water. There are beautiful walks through the temple groves crowning the island, and the cave temple

to the Goddess Benten may be visited at low tide. Its tea-houses
serve fish dinners, and each one commands some specially fine view.
On the opposite beach, at Katase, there is the best surf-bathing.
To return to Yokohama more quickly one may drive to the Fuji-
sawa station and take the train. (Fare 42 *sen* 1st class ; 28 *sen* 2d
class).

Yokosuka is distant from Yokohama twenty-two miles by train
(fare 66 *sen* 1st class ; 44 *sen* 2d class), or, distant fifteen miles by
small steamer (fare 20 *sen*), which leaves the English
YOKOSUKA. Hatoba four times daily. The government arsenal,
navy-yard, dry-docks and ship-yards are at Yokosuka,
and as Japan ranks well as a naval power, there is always something
of interest to be seen. A mile beyond Yokosuka is the grave of
Will Adams, an English pilot, who arrived on a Dutch trading vessel
in 1607, and being able to teach ship-building and other useful arts,
was not allowed to leave the country. Turn to the right from the
landing place, follow the street until it crosses the bridge and then
up the steep road to a stone staircase that leads to the summit of a
hill. The view well rewards one for this walk to Will Adams's grave.

Having his passport ready, the traveler may leave Yokohama
after tiffin, take the Tokaido Railway to Kodzu (fare 93 *sen* 1st class;
62 *sen* 2d class), distant forty-nine miles. A carriage
MIYANOSHITA. or tram will convey him to Yumoto, and a jinrikisha
carry him on to Miyanoshita in time for dinner.
The two large hotels, the Fujiya and Naraiya's, are kept in foreign
style, with excellent table, baths, billiard-rooms, etc. The little
mountain village is full of woodenware and toy shops, the whole
region is wild and picturesque, and the soda and sulphur baths and
the cool bracing air are tonic and exhilarating. Miyanoshita is open
the year round, and in summer its hotels are crowded. To Hakone
Lake, to the Ojigoku (asolfatara) and to Otomitoge Pass are the
favorite jaunts. From Otomitoge the great plain around Fujiyama
lies below one, and it is five miles down to Gotemba, where he may
take the train back to Yokohama, or on to Kioto and Kobe.

Gotemba is the starting point for the ascent of Fujiyama, which
may be made at any time during July or August, when the rest-houses
on the mountain are open, and thousands of pilgrims
TO FUJIYAMA. visit them. The ascent has been made in June and
in September, but guides and coolies deprecate the
risk, and two Englishmen who made the climb in December, 1891,
only kept two coolies with them by main force.
From Gotemba it is seven miles by jinrikisha
to Subashiri and thence five miles by horse or
Kago to Umagayeshi (Turn Back Horse).
The kago is a basket palanquin slung from
a pole carried on the shoulders of two men,
"who trudge with a steady and firm step, as
though they were carrying a jackdaw in a
cage instead of a burly Englishman," says Dr.
Dresser.

From Umagayeshi every one must walk the fifteen miles, through
the wood and over the open lava slopes to the tenth and last rest-
house at the summit. The priest at the summit temple will stamp
staff and clothing and sell a pictured certificate of ascent. The
height of the summit is 12,365 feet above the level of the sea according to Stewart's estimate. From the circle of temples on the crater's

FUJIYAMA.

rim all of five provinces and a great stretch of ocean may be seen.

The first Fuji pilgrim was Sin-fu, a Chinese sage who, in the third century B. C., led a train of six hundred youths and maidens to seek for the Emperor Che-Wang-Te a panacea for immortality to be procured only on the summit of Fujiyama.* The holy band never returned.

The first European to ascend was Sir Rutherford Alcock in 1860, and a foreign woman was later the first of her sex on the summit; as the goddess Fuji-San was known to hate her own sex and to keep devils to fly away with such rash invaders.

The summit may be reached from Umagayeshi in less than six hours, including rests. Coolies carry extra clothing, rubber garments and provisions, and if the pilgrim is to spend the night at any of the rest-houses he should carry a large supply of Keating's powder or oil of pennyroyal. The descent down a shoot of loose cinders to the forest belt is made in less than an hour, and *waraji* or straw sandals tied on over leather shoes will prevent them from being cut to pieces by these sharp cinders. The snow leaves the mountain entirely in mid summer, and the heat and dust on the open lava cone are the greatest discomforts of the trip.

Starting from Yokohama in the morning, one may reach No. 8 station, or even the summit, before night, and, viewing sunrise from the crater's rim, descend and reach Yokohama the following evening.

The railway fare to Gotemba and return, charges for jinrikisha, kago, guide and coolies, lodging, etc., amount altogether to less than ten dollars for each person; and a party of men, who are good climbers and travelers, may lessen this average.

Twenty miles below Kodzu on the coast is Atami, a favorite watering-place, which has sulphur baths and a geyser bubbling at the very edge of the ocean. Sheltered in its little

ATAMI. bay by an amphitheatre of cliffs and mountains, and with the long rollers of the open Pacific sweeping up its beach of golden sand, which is warmed by the subterranean heat, Atami is a winter and early spring resort of great attraction. It is mild, warm, pleasant and sunny there when the worst winter weather is raging at the capital.

As a resort it is in highest favor with the Court and the noble families of Tokio. In returning one may cross the mountains from Atami to Mishima and join the railway on the great plain below Fujiyama.

At Kanozan, across the bay from Yokohama, a foreign hotel, the Yuyukwan, has lately been opened which makes that village, on a mountain summit, a desirable summer resort. From it is obtained the famous view of the "Ninty-nine Valleys." A small steamer leaves Tokio at 8.00 a.m. for Kisaradzu (fare 40 *sen*), jinrikisha from Kisaradzu to the Yuyukwan, 50 *sen*.

* See Nitobe, page 5.

34

VII

The railway from Yokohama to Tokio follows near the shore of Yeddo Bay for its eighteen miles. (Fare 60 *sen* 1st class ; 40 *sen* 2d class ; or round-trip fares $1.20 1st class ; 80 *sen* 2d class.) Trains leave hourly, but the exact sched- **TO TOKIO.** ule may be had from the daily papers. At Omori, half way, the tourist should stop and take the jinrikisha to the Ikegami Temples, a mile and a half distant. These are the head temples of the Nichiren sect of Buddhists. The annual matsuri, or religious festival, occurs on the twelfth and thirteenth of October, and presents a spectacle almost unrivaled in Japan. It is the most popular and picturesque of all the matsuris in the region, but has been fully described elsewhere.*

The train follows the shore of the bay through the Shinagawa suburb and stops at Shinbashi station. Turning to the left, after he passes the wicket, the stranger will find the jinrikisha stand. He may take a check from the jinrikisha bureau at the top of the steps and avoid all trouble of settlements by paying for his runners there. Seventy-five cents a day is the regular charge, but as the distances which a sightseer, shopper, or caller covers are so great, a gratuity is added for a long day's run, or else two coolies are employed. Sanjiro, the famous English-speaking runner, picks and chooses his customers at will, and will serve one as well as a guide, but all his colleagues know the rounds meant when told to *maru maru* (go sight-seeing).

The Club and Seiyoken hotels in the Tsukiji district, near the railway station, and the Imperial **CLUBS,** and Tokio hotels, west of it, are all kept in Euro- **HOTELS AND** pean style. The Senyentei restaurant in Shiba Park, **TEMPLES.** and the Seiyoken in Uyeno Park, are both kept in foreign style ; Fugetsudo, the caterer and confectioner near the station, has a small restaurant where a tiffin or tea may be quickly served.

The British Legation is in Kojimachi, facing the palace moats ; and the United States Legation is in Azabu, west of Shiba Park. Beside his passport, the tourist may secure from his lega- tion tickets for the Hama Rikiu Gardens, an imperial pleasure ground where landscape-gardening has reached its limit. He may also obtain permission to visit the famous garden of the old Mito Yashiki, now the Arsenal, by addressing the

* "Jinrikisha Days in Japan." by Eliza Ruhamah Scidmore. page 114. New York: Harper & Brothers. 1891

Minister of War through his legation. The Imperial Palace in Tokio is not open to sightseers. Only those bidden to its state functions may cross its marble bridge. Through his legation the tourist may obtain permits to visit the Imperial Palace and Nijo Castle at Kioto, and the old castle at Nagoya.

The mortuary temples of the Tokugawa Shoguns at Shiba and Uyeno Parks, are the finest examples of architecture and decoration in Tokio, and the jinrikisha runners will lead to the gateways where entrance to their interiors may be had. A fee of twenty-five *sen* is paid the priest who conducts one through the temple and to the tomb of Hidetada, the Ni Dai Shogun; and the same is paid at Uyeno. On entering a temple, the inner rooms of a shop or tea-house, shoes must always be removed, as the finely-woven, exquisitely-clean straw mats and the polished wooden floors would be hopelessly ruined by the tread of coarse and dirty leather. Hidetada's tomb is very fine, but the most beautiful mortuary chapel, garden and tomb at Shiba are those of the 6th Tokugawa Shogun, "Roku Dai." The bronze doors at the entrance of the tomb are deservedly famous.

At Asakusa Temple shoes are not removed, and that popular Buddhist temple of the masses is best described by Miss Bird, in her "Unbeaten Tracks in Japan." Religion and amusement go hand-in-hand there, and, having paid and prayed, the pilgrim may amuse and enjoy himself in a hundred ways at a thousand booths, shops, theatres, side-shows and restaurants. From an imitation Fujiyama and a mock Eiffel Tower he obtains a bird's-eye view of the city of a million and a half inhabitants which rivals the outlook from the Rond Point of Uyeno Park, from the Kudan Hill, and from the tea-houses at Atagoyama, near Shiba—all widely separated points of view. Great flower shows are always in progress at Asakusa.

There are three government museums in Uyeno Park, and a bazaar for the sale of goods of Tokio manufacture, all of which should be visited. The Zoological Garden contains a good collection of animals, and there is a pleasant drive from that pleasure ground to the Botanical Gardens, passing the buildings of the Imperial University on the way.

Near the Ryogoku Bashi the colony of wrestlers abide, and every spring hold their great tourney. The word *sumo* (wrestler) is sufficient order to the jinrikisha coolie, and if there be a **WRESTLERS AND SHOWS.** show tent open, it is soon declared by long pendant banners and gay standards, and one may watch the obese, overfed champions conduct their struggles on anything but the Westmoreland rules.

The Shintomiza and the Chitose theatre, near Asakusa, all the region around the Asakusa Temple, and the whole length of the Ginza, the Broadway of Tokio, furnish one dramatic, acrobatic amusements, side-show and outdoor entertainment of every kind for the after-dinner hours. Every night is fête night somewhere, and always one will find throngs of happy people between double rows of lanterned and torch-lighted booths, where all the toys, plants, flowers, fruits, confections, commodities, notions and gewgaws tempt and delight the masses. Of such fêtes writes Percival Lowell:

"Whatever these people fashion, from the toy of an hour to the triumphs of all time, is touched by a taste unknown elsewhere. To stroll down the Broadway of Tokio of an evening is a liberal education in every-day art. Two long lines **JAPANESE** of gaily-lighted shops, stretching off into the distance, **SHOPS.** look out across two equally endless rows of torch-lit booths, the decorous yellow gleam of the one contrasting strangely with the demoniacal red flare of the other. As your feet follow your eyes, you find yourself in a veritable shopper's paradise, the galaxy of twinkle resolving into worlds of delight. Nor do you long remain a mere spectator; for the shops open their arms to you. No cold glass reveals their charms only to shut you off. Their wares lie invitingly exposed to the public, seeming to you already half your own. At the very first you come to you stop involuntarily, lost in admiration over what you take to be bric-a-brac. It is only afterwards you learn that the object of your ecstacy was the commonest of kitchen crockery. Next door you halt again, this time in front of some leathern pocketbooks, stamped with designs in colors to tempt you instantly to empty your wallet for more new ones than you will ever have the means to fill. * * * Opposed as stubbornly as you may be to idle purchase at home, here you will find yourself the prey of an acute case of shopping fever before you know it. Nor will it be much consolation subsequently to discover that you have squandered your patrimony upon the most ordinary articles of every-day use.

"If, in despair, you turn for refuge to the booths, you will but have delivered yourself into the embrace of still more irresistible fascinations, for the nocturnal squatters are there for the express purpose of catching the susceptible. The shops were modestly attractive from their nature, but the booths deliberately make eyes at you, and with telling effect. The very atmosphere is bewitching. The lurid smokiness of the torches lends an appropriate weirdness to the figure of the uncouthly-clad peddler who, with the politeness of the arch-fiend himself, displays to an eager group the fatal fascinations of some new conceit. * * * Beyond this lies spread out on a mat a most happy family of curios, the whole of which you are quite prepared to

purchase *en bloc*. * * *

So one attraction fairly jostles its neighbor for recognition from the gay thousands that, like yourself, stroll past in holiday delight. Chattering children in brilliant colors, voluble women and talkative men in quieter but no less picturesque costumes, stream on in kaleidoscopic continuity, and you, carried along by the current, wander thus for miles with the tide of pleasure-seekers, till, late at night, when at last you turn reluctantly homeward, you feel as one does when awakened from some too-delightful dream."*

TOKIO'S greatest fêtes are when the cherry blossoms convert Uyeno Park and the Mukojima river road into such a floral paradise

TOKIO FÊTES.

as no Occidental dreams of, and this April carnival is worth hastening, or delaying long to see. The opening of the river at the end of June is another characteristic and picturesque fête of the capital, when the summer boat-life begins, and the moon viewing in September closes it.

New Year's Day, Declaration Day,† and the Emperor's birthday, November 3d, are great official holidays, and court pageants, military reviews and general decorations and illuminations are made.

There is a great wistaria fête at the Kameido Temple in May, when the ancient vines bear flowers three and four feet in length. Gold-fish as many feet in length live in the temple lake, and may be seen at any season by him who will clap his hands and scatter cakes on the water. From the Seiyoken restaurant in Uyeno Park he may look down upon many acres of blooming lotus in July and August.

In October the greatest chrysanthemum show in the world begins in the Dangozaka quarter, and no flower fancier knows the chrysanthe-

THE CHRYSANTHE- MUM SHOW.

mum and its possibilities until he has seen the marvelous blossoms and the life-size and colossal flowerpieces there. Of that beloved national flower Percival Lowell says:

"The symmetry of its shape well fits it to symbolize the completeness of perfection which the Mikado, the Son of Heaven, mundanely represents. It typifies, too, the fullness of the year. It may be of almost any hue, and within the general limits of a circle of any form. Now it is a chariot wheel with petals for spokes; now a ball of fire with lambent tongues of flame; while another kind seems the button of some natural legion of honor, and still another a pin-wheel in Nature's own day fireworks."

* " The Soul of the Far East," page 114.
† Anniversary of the Declaration of the New Constitution, February 11, 1889.

38

Besides the curio shops on the Nakadori and the Nishi Nakadori there are many similar shops scattered throughout the city.

A guide will quickly arrange for a dinner in Japanese style at some tea-house, and engage jugglers, or *maiko* and *geisha* (professional dancers and singers), to entertain the company between the courses.

In Tokio and in Yokohama are agencies for the sale of the creamy-toned mulberry writing paper manufactured by the government Insatsu-Kioku Paper Mills at Oji. The heavy wall paper, imitating the richest stamped leather, is manufactured at the Insatsu-Kioku works adjoining the Ministry of Finance, but none of it is sold in Japan, all going to agents in foreign countries.

There is no accepted drive or promenade where the great world of Tokio gathers for its afternoon airing, no Rotten Row nor particular boulevard. Any day the Emperor and his suite may pass by, but each spring and autumn the sovereign and the court lend splendor to the review of troops held at the Aoyama or Hibiya parade ground. At the Kudan and Uyeno race tracks high life and sporting circles meet in spring and autumn.

VIII.

Nikko, the site of the most splendid temples in Japan, and a mountain refuge of great popularity in midsummer, is reached by railway in five hours from Tokio. (Fare $2.75 1st class; $1.82 2d class.) On the return one may take jinriki-sha to Utsonomiya and ride for twenty-three miles down an avenue lined with ancient cryptomeria trees. **NIKKO, THE CITY OF TEMPLES.**

Suzuki's hotel, in the village; the new Nikko Hotel across the river adjoining the temple grounds, and Kanaya's hotel in the upper village, will lodge the traveler. In one day he may visit the two great temples and the tombs of the Shoguns, Iyeyasu and Iyemitsu; take the woodland walk around the sacred hill; cross the river by the upper bridge and see the ancient images lining the bank; see the sacred Red Bridge and choose souvenirs in the pretty village shops.

A small admission fee is charged at each temple. A score of writers beside Dr. Dresser have found words inadequate to describe these "shrines as glorious in color as the Alhambra in the days of its splendor, and yet with a thousand times the interest of that beautiful building."

To quote again that poetic word-painter, Percival Lowell:

"At the farther end rises a building, the like of which for richness of effect you have probably never beheld nor even imagined. In front of you a flight of white stone steps leads up to a terrace whose parapet, also of stone, is diapered for half its height and open lattice work the rest. This piazza gives entrance to a building or set

INNER GATE OF IYEMITSU TEMPLE, NIKKO.

of buildings whose every detail challenges the eye. Twelve pillars of snow-white wood sheathed in part with bronze, arranged in four rows, make, as it were, the bones of the structure. The space between the centre columns lies open. The other triplets are webbed in the middle, and connected on the sides and front by grilles of wood and bronze, forming on the outside a couple of embrasures on either hand the entrance, in which stand the guardian Nio, two colossal demons, Gog and Magog. Instead of capitals a frieze bristling with Chinese lions protects the top of the pillars. Above this in place of entablature rise tier upon tier of decoration, each tier projecting beyond the one beneath, and the topmost of all terminating in a balcony which encircles the whole second story. The parapet of this balcony is one mass of ornament, and its cornice another row of lions, brown instead of white. The second story is no less crowded with carving. Twelve pillars make its ribs, the spaces between being filled with elaborate woodwork, while on top rest more friezes, more cornices, clustered with excrescences of all colors and kinds, and guarded by lions innumerable. To begin to tell the details of so multi-faceted a gem were artistically impossible. It is a jewal of a thousand rays, yet whose beauties blend into one, as the prismatic tints combine to white. And then, after the first dazzle of admiration, when the spirit of curiosity urges you to penetrate the centre aisle, lo, and behold it is but a gate! The dupe of unexpected splendor, you have been paying court to the means of approach. It is only a portal after all. For as you pass through you catch a glimpse of a building beyond more gorgeous still. Like in general to the first, unlike it in detail, resembling it only as the mistress may the maid. But who shall convince of charm by enumerating the features of a face! From the tiles of its terrace to the encrusted gables that drape it as with some rich bejeweled mantle, falling about it in the most graceful of folds, it is the very Eastern Princess of a building, standing in the majesty of her court to give you audience.

"A pebbly path, a low flight of stone steps, a pause to leave your shoes without the sill, and you tread in the twilight of reverence upon the moss-like mats within. The richness of its outer ornament, so impressive at first, is, you discover, but prelude to the lavish luxury of its interior. Lacquer, bronze, pigments, deck its ceiling and its sides in such profusion that it seems to you as if art had expanded in the congenial atmosphere, into a tropical luxuriance of decoration, and grew here as naturally on temples as in the jungle creepers do on trees."

And finally, says Dr. Dresser: "I am getting weary of beauty. * * * I am also weary of writing of the beautiful, for I feel that any words that I can use must fail to convey any adequate idea of the conscientiousness of the work, the loveliness of the compositions, the harmoniousness of the colors, and the beauty of the surroundings here before me; and yet the adjectives which I have tried to heap one upon another, in the hope of conveying to the reader what I—an architect and ornamentist—feel when contemplating these matchless shrines, must appear, I am afraid, altogether unreasonable."

THE WALLS OF THE IYEYASU TEMPLE, NIKKO.

Thousands of pilgrims visit the region each summer, and the annual matsuri occurs in September.

It is a pleasant excursion up higher in the mountains to Lake Chiuzenji, the eight miles being made on foot, in saddle or *kago*. Crossing the lake by boat and following the road for six miles, Yumoto, LAKE a favorite watering-place, is reached. There one may CHIUZENJI spend the night and return to Nikko the following AND YUMOTO. day in time for a second visit to the temples, which is much more satisfactory than the first bewildering glimpses.

Returning from Nikko by train the tourist interested in silk culture may change at Oyama, take train for Maebashi and thence by jinrikisha seven miles, reach Ikao, the centre of the Joshu silk district. There are excellent hotels in foreign style and hot mineral baths which attract many of the better class of Japanese who, to cure their ills, spend whole days in the pools with floating tables before them on which they write, play games and eat. The village street is lined with charming little wooden-ware shops; Ikao's confections are renowned; there are magnificent views from every part of the village, and the neighborhood offers many excursions. A good walker, indifferent to a little hardship, may get quite off the beaten track by crossing the mountains to Nikko by the Ashiwokaido, a distance of sixty-eight miles. No one should attempt it without a guide, and ladies not at all.

Rice cultivation is everywhere to be seen in city suburbs, beside railroads and highways, and one soon grows familiar with the flooded fields, the level patches of intensely green spears, or the stacks and festooned fringes of ripened grain.

Tea plantations are seen all along the line of the Tokaido Railway, and in the great tea district south of Kioto. The firing and packing for export may be witnessed at any of the many tea-firing godowns in Yokohama or Kobe.†

Taking train to Awomori at the extreme north end of the island, the tourist may cross to Hokodate and in short excursions reach Aino villages where remnants of the conquered aborigine people of Japan are fast dying out.

IX.

In traveling by railway between Tokio and Kioto, the traveler may make the journey between early morning and midnight of the same day, or break the long ride by stopping over
night at Shidzuoka or Nagoya and seeing these pro- **SHIDZUOKA.**
vincial capitals. There are no sleeping cars, and
in the tourist's favorite seasons, the passenger is not always sure of a whole sofa to himself for the night. At Shidzuoka, the hotel, in foreign style, is directly facing the station. There is an interesting old temple and the remains of the castle walls and moat to interest

† See " Jinrikisha Days in Japan," pages 350-58.

those who stop longer than twelve hours, and the vendors of the airy, bird-cage-like baskets, peculiar to Shidzuoka, have learned to seek out and tempt the tourist the instant he arrives.

There is a twenty minutes' ride in jinrikisha from the station at Nagoya to the foreign hotel in the heart of the city. The great earthquake of October, 1891, so twisted and wrenched

NAGOYA. the great beams of the castle keep that visitors are for the time debarred from ascending its stairways to look out upon the Owari plain and the bay of Owari. The Buddhist temple and the cloisonnee factories are the chief points for sightseers, and the streets and shops show much of Japanese life unaffected by foreign fashions. He who has a real interest in the land and its people will leave the beaten track at Nagoya, and crossing the bay at Yokkaichi, make a pilgrimage to the sacred shrines at Yamada in Ise, the cradle and treasure houses of the Shinto cult. All summer devout pilgrims tramp with jingling staffs through the sacred groves of Ise, and much of old Japan lingers in that province.

CASTLE AT NAGOYA.

X.

The Canadian Pacific steamers' regular ports of call are Yokohama, Kobe, Nagasaki, Shanghai and Hong Kong.

The tourist may proceed by frequent local steamer **AT KOBE.** to Kobe and through the Inland Sea to Nagasaki.

Within twenty-four hours after leaving Yokohama such steamers enter the Inland Sea and anchor off Kobe, the foreign settlement adjoining the ancient town of Hiogo. The tourist may also reach Kobe by the Tokaido Railway in less time (fare $10.74 1st class; $7.16 2d class), or he may stop off at Nagoya, cross Lake Biwa, visit Kioto, Nara and Osaka before taking ship again.

Kobe-Hiogo, the second export city of the empire, with a population now exceeding 90,000, has a most picturesque setting, and at night the harbor and hillsides look as if purposely illuminated. The Hiogo Hotel on the Bund, the Oriental, the Hotel des Colonies and the German Club Hotel are excellently kept in foreign style. The Consulates, banks and shipping agencies are all in the Concession, between the Hatoba and the railway. The Kobe Club is on the Recreation Ground, or foreign park, just in the rear of the Custom House. The Boat Club further east, and fronting on the beach, has bathing barge, dressing rooms and boat-houses.

The sights of the town are the Nanko Temple and the Shinkoji Temple in Hiogo; the Ikuta Temple, the Nunobiki waterfalls, and the raised river bed, the Minatogawa, which is park and pleasure ground for the Japanese community.

The Motomachi, or main street, is a lane of delight in the way of attractive shops.

No passport is required to visit Arima or Osaka. The former is a mountain village sixteen miles inland where nearly all the bamboo baskets for the foreign trade are manufactured. Arima has also medicinal springs and is a fashionable place of resort for the rheumatic and ailing, Hideyoshi having given it vogue centuries ago. Its picturesque streets and surroundings, its shops and workrooms easily entertain one for a day. Returning to Kobe, the traveler may take *kago*, or walk, to the top of Rokusan, and there enjoy a matchless view of mountain, sea and plain, descend the steep road to Sumiyoshi station and take train five miles to Kobe.

Osaka is distant twenty miles from Kobe by rail (fare 60 *sen* 1st class; 40 *sen* 2d class. Return tickets $1.20 1st class; 80 *sen*

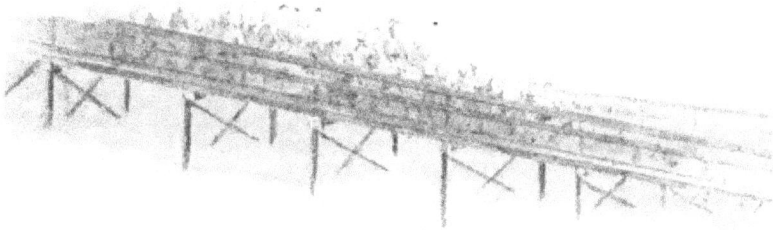

2d class). Trains leave hourly for Osaka and at longer intervals for Kioto, which is twenty-seven miles beyond Osaka.

The traveler may visit that second city of the empire, variously called the Venice, the Glasgow and the Chicago of Japan. Formerly it was the military capital. Much of Japanese history has been made within its castle and even foreign writers have made its romances known.* The last acts of the Shogunate were played there, and with the surrender of 1868 the Restoration began. Its 361,694 people, its three hundred bridges, its great temples and workshops are all matters of boastful pride to those prosperous citizens.

In one day the traveler can easily see its more important sights: the Castle, the Tennoji Temple and Pagoda, the Mint, Arsenal, Hongwanji Temple, the Hakku Butsu, or commer-

THE SIGHTS OF OSAKA. cial baazar, the theatre, street, and the large curio shops. The Hakku Butsu is open at night, and condensing all the shops and factories of the town in that one place, one may review industrial Osaka by electric light. The labyrinthine bazaar is the delight of the Japanese, and they love to follow its tortuous mazes without ever an impulse to turn back. There are small ones without number in every theatre region, and each city has a large bazaar under government control, where goods marked in plain figures are sold for a small commission. There one may find everything useful and useless, the necessities and the luxuries of life, newest inventions, antiques, curios and much that one may never come across elsewhere.

The great silk shops contain the richest fabrics loom and hand can produce, but trade in them proceeds on leisurely Japanese lines, highly entertaining to one who has time at command, and maddening to the hurried tourist, watch and time table in hand.

Jiutei's Hotel, on an island in the river, will lodge and cheer the tourist after European methods.

XI.

No traveler fails to visit Kioto, the soul and centre, the heart of old Japan, and most fascinating city of the Empire.

If he has not a general passport, including Kioto, obtained through a Tokio legation, the

KIOTO. traveler may secure a permit to visit Kioto through his Consul at Kobe. A citizen of the United States may apply directly to the Kobe Kencho himself, but

* "The Usurper. A Tale of the Siege of Osaka Castle." By Judith Gautier, Paris.

citizens of all other nationalities are held amenable to stricter discipline by their consuls, and obliged to proceed through them in all official matters.

It is possible to go to Kioto by a morning train, see several temples, tiffin at Yaami's, visit the Palace and Castle, do a little shopping, and return to ship at night, if one has a good guide and is limited to that one day on shore. The professional guides are registered at the Kobe hotels. Failing to secure one, the flying tourist may telegraph Yaami to send an English-speaking boy to the train at Kioto. He may visit the two Hongwanji temples, the Dai Butsu and Chioin temples before reaching the hotel whose proprietors were formerly guides and knowing what the tourist wants to or ought to see, can quickly put him in the way of it. The Kioto Hotel in the level plain of the city is also kept in foreign style, but Yaami's is historic ground—one of the institutions of Japan—and all must seek its verandas for the panorama of the city.

Of the great temples, the Chionin is a hillside neighbor of Yaami's, and its bronze bell, eighteen feet in length, shakes the whole hotel when it rings. This, with the Kiomidzu, Dai Butsu, Sanjiusangendo and the two Hongwanjis, are **TEMPLES.** the great Buddhist shrines. The Higashi Hong-wanji is the largest temple in Japan, covering 52,380 square feet

THE JUNK PINK TREE AT THE KINKAKUJI, KIOTO.

of ground, and rising to a height of 126 feet. When completed. its interior will be the most splendid in the empire. The Gion, the great Shinto shrine, lies at the foot of Yaami's hill.

After an entire morning of temples, an afternoon may be agreeably given to the great silk shops where English speaking clerks are always found.

The Palace and the Nijo Castle, permits to visit which must be obtained through a Tokio legation, and the Kinkakuji (a small suburban palace, now a monastery), will will occupy another morning, and curio shops will beguile that afternoon. The Kinkakuji (the gold-covered pavilion) and the Ginkakuji (the silver-covered pavilion) are two model landscape gardens of Japan, after which classic designs half the minature paradises of the land are arranged. Both monasteries contain famous pictures and screens. The Kinkakuji has a special fame in possessing an ancient pine tree trained in the shape of a junk in one of its courts; and the Ginkakuji holds the first and oldest ceremonial tea-house in Japan.

Every visitor should walk the two bewitching streets of Teapot Hill: the one, a half-mile lane of china shops leading to the Kiomidzu temple, and the other conducting to the Nishi Otani temple. Nor should he miss the lane leading through a bamboo grove that joins the two streets. nor yet the shop-lined staircase that takes him to the foot of the Yasaka pagoda.

A favorite excursion is to Takao, on the Oigawa, where the traveler takes flatboat and shoots the rapids of that river, and resumes jinrikisha at Arashiyama, a southwestern suburb of Kioto. If not too many, the jinrikishas may be taken in the boat or another boat hired for them. Three or four *yen* are asked for each boat, and the passage is made in less than two hours. Luncheon may be taken from the hotel, or the tourist may feast at the Arashiyama tea-house. Arashiyama is the Kioto synonym for cherry blossoms, and all the geishas in the empire have a dance that tells of cherry blossoming by the Oigawa. In April these hillsides rival the rosy slopes of Maruyama, where that enormous old cherry tree at the foot of Yaami's lane has drawn worshipping crowds for three hundred years. While it blooms a gala season reigns and the great dancing fête, the Miakodori, goes on at the neighboring geisha school.

The visitor may vary his experience by making the journey from Kioto to Nara by jinrikisha. It is but twenty-six miles, the roads

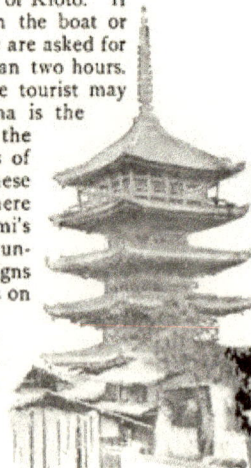

are perfect, the country picturesque, the wayside full of interest, and all the ground historic. For a jinrikisha with two men to Nara one pays $2.50. The road runs through the famous Yamashiro tea district, and Uji, the chief town, is **NARA.** always fragrant with the toasting leaf. The Phoenix temple near Uji was reproduced at the Chicago Exposition, 1893. The Musashino tea-house on the hill between the two temple grounds, and the Oya in the town, are the best tea-houses at Nara.

The Dai Butsu Temple contains a bronze statue of Buddha fifty-three and a half feet in height, and at the Kasuga Temple the young Shinto priestesses will perform the sacred dance after the visitor has made a gift of one or more *yen* to the temple. The tame deer that roam these temple grounds, and even the village streets, will come at call and eat from one's hand.

There is a railway from Nara to Osaka, and reversing the trip, the traveler, who has a passport for Nara, may run up from Osaka in a little over an hour, give two or four hours to the temple grounds, and if the guide has provided a tiffin, picnic at one of the picturesque *tateba* or wayside tea sheds among the ancient trees and lanterns.

XII.

Speed is not a consideration for the voyage between Kobe and Nagasaki, a distance of 389 miles. The way lies in and out among the islands of the Inland Sea, the most picturesque stretch of enclosed ocean : an ideal, poetic region, where even the huge steamship seems to float enchanted, and all the sea and sky and shores are a day-dream. Silently the ship threads the narrowest of channels ; square-sailed junks float by ; towns, villages, castles, temples, forests, cultivated vales and terraced hills, sharply-cut peaks and low-running mountain chains succeed one another for a whole day.

The railway is completed from Kobe to Hiroshima, the naval station in the Inland Sea, and near it is the sacred island of Miajima, with its *torii* built far out in the water, all its shores lined with stone lanterns, and tame deer roaming among its wistaria-entangled groves as at Nara. No one has ever been born nor has died on this sacred island, and its summer matsuris are feasts of lanterns and of picturesqueness outdoing those of all other shrines.

Those who would cruise in this enchanting sea may easily charter at Kobe small steamers, accommodating from five to ten persons, for $50 and $60 a week, the lessee providing coal and provisions. Six weeks is the usual time given to a leisurely cruise in the Inland Sea, but in these days tourists boast of doing it all within a fortnight.

At Shimonoseki the ship passes the last narrow gateway and goes out to the open ocean for a short stretch, after which its route is close inshore, behind a chain of islands. Fishing boats dot the water, villages and terraced fields **TO NAGASAKI.** break the shore-line, and the Arched Rock is always pointed out. The ship threads a narrow entrance and passes up the long fiord to Nagasaki, a harbor ranking with Sydney and Río de Janeiro for picturesqueness. Men-of-war are always at their anchorage-ground, and the harbor busy with other craft. The Nagasaki sampans are nearest to gondolas, and their covered cabins declare the frequent rains which make such protection necessary. Mail steamers, having to coal there, always allow their passengers time to explore the town and the temple-crowded hillside.

The Bellevue and Smith hotels are near the Hatoba, and the

THE WATER GATE AT MIAJIMA TEMPLES—INLAND SEA.

Club is on the Bund, at the foot of the hillside set apart for the foreign residents.

The O'Suwa is the great temple and is surrounded by a public park. Near it is the Koransha, or general bazaar, a smaller edition of Osaka's great industrial aggregation.

The porcelain, or Deshima, bazaar is housed in buildings erected by the Dutch in the long ago, when they lived as prisoners on this walled and bridge-guarded island—all for the sake of a trade monopoly. The wares made at Imari, Arita and Hirado, in this same

province of Hizen, are brought to Deshima by junk, and one has choice of many beautiful designs rarely met in the foreign market.

The carving and fashioning of tortoise-shell articles occupies many artisans, and one may look into many shops where the busy workers are sawing, cutting, carving and polishing the shell. Much imitation shell is palmed off upon the unitiated, but one may choose his shell and watch his work begun, and, if he stays in port any time, follow its daily progress.

Pierre Loti has so charmingly described many Nagasaki scenes in "Mme. Chrysantheme," that its readers will easily identify his *locale*. In Nagasaki begins that pretty little romance, "The Viewing of the Cherry Blossoms."

Many visitors have been tempted to linger at Nagasaki, visit the Hot Springs a few miles inland, the quaint villages along the deeply indented coast, and, having passports, see Kumamoto's fine old castle, and Kagoshima, capital of the province of Satsuma.

XIII.

At Nagasaki the zealous traveler who would see North China and a little of Korea may diverge from the route of the Canadian Pacific steamers. He may also take ship there for Vladivostock, the terminus of the trans-Siberian railway, should he prefer a land route to Europe.

Embarking in a Nippon Yusen Kaisha steamer he may visit Fusan and Gensan on the east coast of Korea, and, stopping at Chemulpo, go by horse, sedan or boat on the river Han, twenty-six miles inland, to the capital, Seoul. There is a Japanese hotel in foreign style—the Dai Butsu—at Chemulpo. The proprietor will arrange for the journey and confide the tourist to the care of the Japanese tea house in Seoul.

The sights of Seoul, other than its picturesque street life, are few and far between. One looks at the eight gateways in the city wall—which are the gates and walls of Peking in miniature—at the palace gates, the marble pagoda **IN SEOUL** and the bell tower in the city. Without the walls there is the boulder image of Buddha to the northwest ; the temple

and tomb of Queen Chung at the southwest; the temple to the Chinese God of War in the same suburb, and the village of Buddhist priests northeast of the city. Permission may sometimes be obtained from the Foreign Office to visit the abandoned palace, whose neglected buildings and pleasure grounds give an idea of the occupied palace. At rare intervals the king passes through the streets of the city, and the procession accompanying him is not like anything else to be seen in this century—a pageant unchanged in details since the middle ages.

The streets are filthy, the houses mean and wretched, the people indolent, poor and unambitious; a crushed and spiritless race, who for centuries paid tribute to China and Japan to be let alone.

SOUTH GATE AT SEOUL.

From Chemulpo the steamers next go to Chefoo, the watering-place and summer resort for the foreign residents in China, and the chief port of the rich province of Shantung.

CHEFOO. From the Taku forts at the mouth of the Peiho River, Tien Tsin is distant twenty-five miles in air line, but by the tortuous course of the muddy river it is sixty miles. The Globe and the Astor hotels are on the river banks at Tien Tsin. After seeing the interesting native city, the walls of the viceroy's yaamen and the few sights of Tien Tsin, the trip to Peking may be undertaken.

A Chinese guide or boy can be engaged at either hotel who will make all the arrangements for the trip, engage the boats, buy the provisions, cook and serve them, lead one about Peking, to the Great Wall and the Ming Tombs. He is **PEKING.**
paid fifty cents a day, and no other charges or allow-
ances are made except as a present at the end of his service. Bedding for use on the boat and in the trip to the Great Wall may be rented of the hotel at Tien Tsin. A house-boat, with its crew of oarsmen and trackers, can be had for eight or ten dollars (Mexican), and by paying fifty cents apiece extra trackers may be had who will walk all night and get the boat up the ninety miles of river to Tung-chow in forty-eight hours. In returning, the boat trip has been made in twenty hours, but thirty hours is the average time. On horseback the actual traveling time is less, but one must then pass a night at a Chinese inn, which is not always desirable. From Tungchow to Peking there are thirteen miles which the tourist passes over in the springless Peking cart, on horse, or in sedan chair.

At Peking there is the excellent Hotel de Peking, kept in foreign style, where every comfort is secured, and every information and assistance given the visitor. The foreign legations are all near by in the one quarter in the Tartar City, within the second wall, and the Liu li Chang, the booksellers' street, where the silk and curio, and the shops generally attractive to the tourists are centered, is near the gate.

One may use bank-notes in Peking, and drafts are cashed at the hotel, but otherwise he pays in *cash*, the round brass coins with a hole in the middle, of which nine hundred make one Mexican dollar. Prices are also quoted to him in *taels* and *sycees*, the latter lumps of silver whose value is determined by weight at each transaction. The *tael* averages in value at $1.35 Mexican.

At several places in the neighborhood of the legations one may, by giving the guards a couple of hundred *cash*, mount the wall, walk there undisturbed, and get a view of the city's different quarters. Within the first or outer wall, thirty **ON**
miles in circumference, is the Chinese City, within **THE WALLS.**
the next circle is the Tartar City, then the Imperial City and the Purple Forbidden City, where the yellow-tiled palace roofs of the Emperor's habitation show above the trees of the park.

In Peking streets Chinese, Manchus, Mongols from the desert, Thibetans, Koreans and every people of Asia jostle together, camel trains, carts, mule-litters, sedans and wheelbarrows crowd the way, and the din and the picturesqueness confuse and bewilder one.

The sights of Peking are lessening in number each year because of the authorities closing show places to foreigners. The Summer Palace, without the walls, destroyed by the French in 1861, is now being rebuilt, and is closed to visitors. The Temple of Heaven, where the Emperor annually worships, was burned a few years since, but its ruins and the other temples within its park are interesting. The Confucian

Temple, the Hall of Classics and the Examination Hall, where the students assemble every year to strive for rank and honors, are also to be seen. The old observatory on the walls, the Mohammedan mosque, the Catholic cathedral and college, the foreign mission establishments and the Lamasery are other places to be visited. There are 1500 priests at the Lamasery, and one must not only bribe largely to gain admittance, but usually pay to get out. The tourist should by no chance go out alone or without his Chinese boy.

It is a three days' trip to visit the Great Wall of China, returning by the way of the tombs of the Ming emperors. The trip is made in **THE** mule litters, which are rented at the rate of one and **GREAT WALL** a half Mexican dollars a day. Outside of Peking all **OF CHINA.** payments are made in *cash*. At the inns only the bare room is supplied, the traveler providing his own bedding and food. The Chinese pay 150 *cash* for the night's lodging, the foreigner usually pays 500 *cash*, including tips. A hard and fast bargain must be made before entering the inn, and the landlord will relent before the obdurate traveler can go many steps away. At Kalgan and Cha Tao, on the other side of the Great Wall, are good inns. A two-mule cart for the servant and luggage is provided at the rate of two Mexican dollars for each day. The splendid tombs of the Ming emperors are visited on the return from the Great Wall, and also the temples among the hills where the foreign legations are housed in midsummer.

The average cost of the trip from Tien Tsin to Peking and return, including the boats, carts, litters and one week's stay at the Hotel de Peking, is put at one hundred Mexican dollars for each person. The trip to Peking affords more novelty, strangeness and incident than any other on the coast, and no one who can command the two or three weeks' time should miss taking it. May and October, the latter especially, are the best months, as the summers are intensely hot and dry, the winters cold, and there is a rainy season in spring, when the streets are in their worst condition.

XIV.

When the Canadian Pacific steamers have stopped at Kobe and threaded the Inland Sea, but a day intervenes from Nagasaki when **YOKOHAMA TO** across the turbid waters of the Yellow Sea there **CHINA.** shows a low brown line, the outermost edge, the farthest rim of the old, mysterious continent of Asia, the real Cathay. Nearer still, trees show like a mirage on the water; then masts of ships and trails of smoke tell of the unseen river winding behind those trees. Junks with laced brown sails go by, huge eyes painted at the bows, for "If no have eye, how can see go?" and dirty, fierce-visaged, pig-tailed crews peer from the litter of matting and bamboo poles. Along the banks are high-walled villages, and the smooth-skinned water buffaloes wallow in the mud below them. The fields are so dotted with round bake-oven graves as to look like a gigantic prairie-dog town, and toilers are everywhere.

The arms of the signal station at the mouth of the Yang-tse Kiang wave, and the telegraph carries the news of the ship's arrival to Shanghai, and launches start to meet it at the Woosung Bar. This is the "Heavenly Barrier," which the Chinese made more effectual than ever, during the French war of 1884, by sinking stone-loaded junks across all but one narrow shallow channel. Twenty years ago there was a railway from Woosung thirteen miles to Shanghai, but the Chinese bought it at a great advance, tore up the rails and threw them with the locomotives into the river.

Approached from the river, this largest foreign settlement of the Far East, the commercial capital of North China presents an imposing appearance. Massive six-story stone buildings front the long Bund, and the compounds of the **SHANGHAI**. United States, Japanese and German Consulates are aligned on the Hongkew side, the old American Settlement. Across the creek bridge are the public gardens, the park surrounding the British Consulate and the commercial heart of the city. Further up the water front, the *quais* and *rues* of the French Settlement, the blue and white signs at each street corner might be corners of Paris itself.

The Astor House and the Hotel des Colonies are the leading hotels. The Club is on the Bund in the English Settlement, and there is the Country Club a few miles out on the Bubbling Well Road, to which ladies belong as well as men, where every one who is any one meets for summer tennis, the afternoon dances, theatricals and balls of the winter season. The spring and autumn races of the Jockey Club attract crowds from all the outports, and much money changes hands. Shanghai social life is formal, exacting, elaborate and extravagant.

The local sights and shows are easily seen in a day. No matter how warm the former friendship may have been, or how powerful the letters of introduction, never ask a resident of a Chinese port to accompany you to a native city; nor talk to him about the excursion afterwards. The resident may tell you that he has never been in the Chinese city; or that he went once ten or twenty years ago. His compradore or house boy will find a friend, or the ever-ready cousin, to act as guide. Entering by the north gate, at the end of the French Settlement, the visitor may balance himself on one of the passenger wheelbarrows and be trundled around the walls to the west or south gate, and then walk through the city to the north gate. He will see the streets of silk, fur, china and other shops, and such swarms of people in the seven-feet wide thoroughfares and side crevices, as support the estimate of 400,000 inhabitants. He must see the Mandarins' Club, or tea garden, the jewelers' guild hall, where there is a continuous auction, and the temple in the midst of a serpentine pond approached by many crooked bridges. Around the pond are outdoor jugglers, fortune tellers, story tellers, menders, barbers and dentists plying their trades, and the din of voices and crowding of the people soon drive him on.

In the foreign city there are handsome shops on Honan Road and the Maloo. There is a Chinese theatre in the quarter near the city walls, and gorgeous costuming is the redeeming point in its deafening dramas. Many Chinese prefer to dwell in that corner of the foreign settlement, where they are amenable to foreign laws and a just taxation, and where offenses are tried in the Mixed Court, which is composed of a Chinese magistrate sitting with two members of the consular board. Rich Chinese come to Shanghai from all the back provinces to spend their money.

The three drives of Shanghai are out the Bubbling Well Road and back, out the Sickaway Road and back, and down the river to the Point and back. Very interesting is a trip by house-boat through the network of rivers, creeks and canals that cover the country. On the boat one lives as luxuriously as on shore, and Shanghai is an epicure's and sybarite's abode.

Notice of the departure of steam launches for Woosung are always posted at the consulates, hotels and club, and information of such departures may be had from the agents of the Canadian Pacific Company's agents, Messrs. Adamson. Bell & Co., whose offices adjoin the club.

There is no government post-office department in China. Each consulate has a post-office of its **POSTAL AR-** own in Shanghai, and **RANGEMENTS.** sells its own postage stamps and despatches mails.

From Shanghai a most interesting trip may be made up the Yang-tse River, one of the world's greatest streams, which rises in the high plains of Thibet, known as "The Roof of the World," and flows for three thousand miles to the sea.

Luxuriously appointed steamers run between Shanghai and the great tea port of Hankow, touching on **TEA** the way at Chinkiang, **DISTRICTS.** Kiukiang and Nankin, and traversing a carefully cultivated garden all the way. Each town has its interesting pagodas and temples ; the river banks present an unceasing panorama of native life, and the water populations add to the picturesqueness and interest. Each town has its specialties in artistic products : silks, silverware, fans, porcelain and faience, and the black tea crop of the empire is raised and cured along this river. Russian and English buyers take nearly all

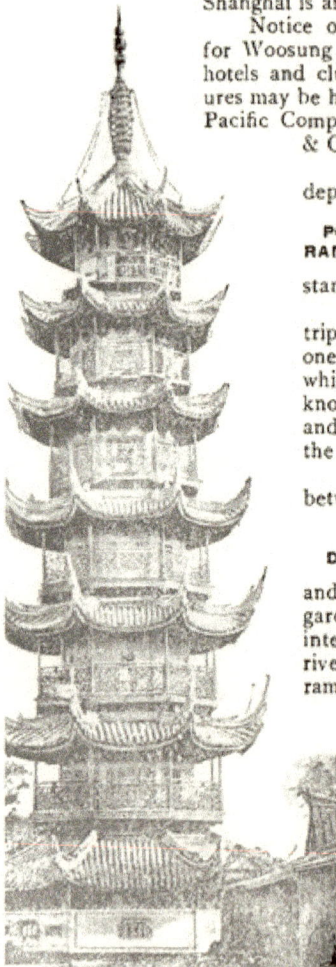

of the Hankow tea and little goes to the United States or Canada, where the oolongs and greener teas of South China and of Japan are chiefly consumed. At Hankow the traveler may take steamer for Ichang still further up the river, from which he may easily reach the famous gorge of the Yang-tse and the first and second rapids, a succession of stupendous cañons through which the great stream races madly.

A sportsman will find the Chinese house-boat the epitome of comfort and luxury, and while sailing and tracking along the upper reaches of the river may treat himself to the finest pheasant shooting in the world. Wild boars abound in the hills near Chinkiang and at other places, and the natives usually welcome the hunters who destroy these depredators of their fields and flocks. The recent anti-foreign riots are warning, however, that the tourist should be well-informed before leaving foreign settlements on any hunting trip.

At Foochow there is the Chinese arsenal and navy yard, and usually some of its European-built men-of-war are to be seen. The river life will interest the waiting voyagers, but shops and specialties are few. The villas of the foreign **FOOCHOW.** residents are hidden in the dense foliage of the hillside. All that hill is covered with graves, and at night the fitful glow of the chair-bearers' lamps among the shadows is strangely weird.

At Amoy there is a picturesque, junk-crowded harbor. In the season loads of tea are constantly arriving from Tamsui and other ports on the hardly-explored island of Formosa, whose pirates and savages make its name a reproach **AMOY.** along the China coast. From orchards up the river come the choicest pumeloes, that most delicious of citrus fruits, which, transplanted, as the shaddock, in the western hemisphere, greatly deteriorates. Amoy pumeloes and the Amoy grass cloth are both superior specialties of the place.

XV.

A blue, blue sea, a barren, brown coast, mountains of burnt rock rising sheer from the exquisite sapphire waters, and, slipping through that veritable needle's eye of **HONG KONG.** the Lymoon Pass, the big, white steamer sweeps into the splendid amphitheatre of Hong Kong harbor, a watery arena thronged with merchantmen and men-of-war of all nations.

Steam launches carry the cabin passengers ashore, and sampans swarm by hundreds, each boat manned by a shrill-voiced woman, who steers, sculls, cooks, manages her children, drives the bargains, and, with her sister boatwomen, chatters incessantly.

Situated on the steep slope of a mountain, Hong Kong, as it rises from the sea, and terrace by terrace climbs the eighteen hundred feet to the summit of the Peak, is most imposing and beautiful. Again, the white houses seem to be slipping down the bold hillside and spreading out at the water's edge in a frontage of more than three miles. The lines of two viaducts—the Bowen and Kennedy Roads, as those high promenades are named for two favorite governors of the colony—draw white coronals around the brow of the mountains, and terraced roads band the hillside with long white lines. All the luxuriant green of the slopes is due to man's agency, and since the island was ceded to England, in 1841, afforestation has been the great work and a miracle wrought. A cable road communicates with the Peak, and at night, when the harbor is bright with myriad lights and trails of phosphorence, and the whole slope glows and twinkles with electricity, gas and oil, the lights of the cable cars are fiery beads slipping up and down an invisible cord.

The city of Victoria, on the island of Hong Kong, is a British colony all to itself, with a colonial governor and staff maintaining a **VICTORIA CITY.** small court and a high social tribunal in its midst. **HONG KONG** It is also the naval station for the British Asiatic fleet, and the docks, arsenal and foundries in the colony and on the opposite Kowloon shore furnish every munition and requirement for war or peace. A large garrison of troops further declares British might, and Hong Kong, the Gibraltar of the East, is an impregnable fortress, and a safeguard to all Asia.

The length of the island of Hong Kong is eleven miles, and its width varies from two to four miles. There are less than 10,000 Europeans in the colony, but a Chinese population of 200,000 has settled around them, although really confined to the western end of the lower levels of the town. A jinrikisha ride down the Praya and the Queen's Road will convince one that the figures of the Chinese population are put too low, if anything. Over 20,000 Chinese live on the harbor-boats besides.

Landing at Pedder's Wharf, the traveler is almost at his hotel door, unless he should arrive during summer, when the hotel at the Peak will be his refuge. One entrance of the Hong Kong Hotel is on Queen's Road, and near it is the Clock Tower, from which all distances are measured. The Hong Kong Club, the German Club, and the Luisitano or Portuguese Club, the Post-Office, and the Hong Kong and Shanghai Bank are all in the immediate neighborhood of the Clock Tower. From that point westward there is a continuous arcade of shops wherein all the arts and industries of South China are exhibited, and one may buy silks, crapes, ivory, lacquer, porcelain, carved teakwood and bamboo wares all the way.

The streets swarm with a motley crowd—Jews, Turks, Mohammedans, Europeans, Hindoos, Javanese, Japanese, Malays, Parsees, Sikhs, Cingalese, Portuguese, half-castes, and everywhere the hard-featured Chinese coolies, carrying poles, buckets, baskets and sedans, or trotting clumsily before a more clumsy jinrikisha. An Indian *ayah*, swathed in white, descends the long stairway of a side street; a Sikh policeman stands statuesque and imperial at a corner; a professional mender, with owlish spectacles, sits by her baskets of rags, darning and patching; a barber drops his pole and boxes and begins to operate upon a customer; rows of coolies sitting against some greasy wall submit their heads to one another's friendly attentions ; a group of pig-tailed youngsters play a sort of shuttlecock with their feet ; peddlers split one's ears with their yells ; firecrackers sputter and bang their appeals to joss ; and from the harbor comes the boom of naval salutes for some arriving man-of-war, the admiral, governor, or a consul paying ship visits.   Such, the constant, bewildering panorama of Queen's Road, the Praya and other thoroughfares, busiest and most cosmopolitan of highways, where the East and the West touch hands—Asia, Australia, Oceanica, Europe and America meet and mingle unconcernedly.

The traveler should see the City Hall and its museum, and take a jinrikisha ride past the barracks to the Race Course in Happy Valley, and visit the Jewish, Parsee, Mohammedan, Anglican and Catholic cemeteries which surround the great oval pleasaunce.   Race week is in February, and is the gala-time of the Hong Kong year.

The grounds about Government House and the Botanical Gardens are the pride of the colony, and banyan-shaded roads, clumps of palms, blooming mimosas, and the wealth of strange luxurious growths, give the tropical setting to every scene.   There is a handsome cathedral below Government House.

To ascend to the higher roads one is carried up those stone or cement staircases of side streets in sedan or hill chairs.   There is a regular tariff of fares, but there is always a discussion at settlement.   No one should attempt to underpay a coolie.   To pay the exact fare generally rouses protest, and to underpay them brings bedlam about one's ears Jinrikishas are supposed to be fifteen cents an hour, or fifty cents a day.   Chairs cost ten cents an hour for each bearer, or twenty cents an hour altogether.   The completion of the cable road to the peak has fortunately done away with much of the chair-riding.

The universal pigeon-English is understood, but a small vocabulary of Chinese words suffices for sedan conversation, as

Be quick, hurry up.	*Fie tee.*
Be careful, look out.	*See sum.*
Come here.	*Liee ne shu.*
Don't do that.	*M-ho tso.*
Stop.	*Man-man.*
Wait a little.	*Tongue yut sum.*
That will do.	*Tos tuck lok.*

More often the bearers rap the poles for one to sit still and keep the balance evenly, or to sit more towards one side or the other. The passenger raps the poles when he wishes to stop, and raps the right or the left pole as he may wish to be set down at one or the other side of the street.

One quickly picks up a few words of pigeon-English, and finds *maskee* for all right, go ahead, agreed, never mind, etc., a most useful word.   *Top side* for up-stairs ; *pidgin* for business, affairs, concerns ; *chop chop* for right away, quickly ; *chow-chow,* or simply *chow,* for food ; *piece* for thing or article ; *side* for place, region, home, country, etc., *catch* for fetch, carry, get, bring and buy, are the most commonly used in one's hearing, and are so quickly adopted in speech that at first one cannot utter a correct English phrase, owing to the corrupting spell of " pidgin."

XVI.

In two hours one may go from Hong Kong to Macao, a three-century-old Portuguese town on the mainland, see its ancient forts, the gardens and grotto where Camoens wrote **WAYS OF LOCOMOTION.** his poems; watch the white and Chinese gamblers in this Monte Carlo of the Far East; view the loading of opium cargoes; rest at an excellent hotel, and enjoy the sea baths.

One day is quite enough for the ordinary traveler to give to Canton sights and sounds. The night boat from Hong Kong will carry him the ninety miles up the Pearl River to that **MACAO.** city of three million inhabitants, and by daylight the din of that many voices will reach his ears like the roar of an angry sea. There is now a hotel on the Shameen, but formerly, unless he had been invited to the home of one of the foreign residents, the traveler lived on the steamer, changing from night boat to day boat, as each came and went.

The dean of the corps of professional guides or a less distinguished cicerone, will present his card upon the arrival of the steamer, and in single file the procession of sedan chairs follows such a leader through the streets, across the city and over an established route which gives a glimpse of every quarter of Canton.

A bridge with closed gates and guards leads to the Shameen, an Arcadian island where the small colony of foreign residents dwell. The Cantonese are not well disposed toward foreigners, and the visitor is warned not to resent any unpleasant remarks or gestures.

In turn one visits the Temple of Five Hundred Genii; the Water Clock in the temple on the walls; the Temple of Horrors, with a courtyard full of fortune tellers and beggars; the Execution Ground, Examination Hall, and the five-story pagoda on the city walls, where the guide will find chairs and table, and set forth the luncheon brought from the steamer or hotel. Returning across the city, one visits the Flowery Pagoda, the ruin of a once splendid marble structure; the old English Yaamen, where the first foreign legation was housed in 1842; the Temple of the Five Genii, the Magistrates' Court, the City Prison, and the Green Tea Merchants' Guild Hall, and returns in time for tea, and a walk through the quiet, banyan-shaded avenues and along the Bund of the Shameen.

The water life of Canton, with the thousands of boats upon which many thousands are born, live, marry and die, a separate class and clan from the landsmen, is always in sight and **CANTON.** sound. The river banks are fringed deeply with these floating homes, and the network of creeks throughout the city holds them as well.

Between the temples one sees the panorama of the open shops, streets of silk and jade and jewelers' shops; weavers' dens and gold-

beaters' caves; shoe shops, cabinet shops, meat and cook shops on either side. Unknown cookery simmers, sputters and scents the air. Dried ducks hang by half-yard-long necks, and a queer flat bit of dried meat declares itself by the long thin tail curled like a grape tendril, to be the rat. The rat is in the market everywhere, alive in cages, fresh or dried on meat-shop counters, and dried ones are often bought as souvenirs of a day in Canton and proof of the often denied rat story. Theatres are many; shops of theatrical wardrobes are endless in one quarter; dealers in old costumes abound, and there are pawn shops and curio shops without end.

The law allows no street to be less than seven feet in width, and some do not exceed it. Down these narrow lanes, with matted awnings overhead, between swinging black, gold and vermilion signboards, the people swarm. Two chairs can barely pass. To turn some sharp corners the poles are run far into the shops, and when a mandarin's chair or mounted escort appears, one is hustled into an open shop front, and is not safe then from the bumping and brushing of the train. It is a most bewildering, dazing, fatiguing day. While the boat slips down the river, past the French cathedral and the busy Whampoa anchorage, out between quiet and level fields, one can hardly remember all the sights. But he dreams of this city of Oriental riches and barbaric splendor, the city of the greatest wealth and the direst poverty, and he sees again the narrow, seething thoroughfares, the blaze of gold and vermilion, the glitter and glow of showy interiors, where if the Queen of Sheba did not live, she certainly went a-shopping.

From Hong Kong the sea ways diverge like the spokes of a wheel to all the ends of the earth, and the traveler may take ship to any country of the globe. Between him and India lie the Straits

Settlements, Siam and Ceylon. Java, with its wonders of nature, the ruins of the greatest temples in the world, the monuments and relics of a past civilization, attracts more travelers, **TOURS FROM** archæologists and botanists each winter, and the **HONG KONG.** completion of a railway system makes it possible to travel quickly and with some comfort through its steaming forests and scorching plains. The accepted guide-book for Java is "The Australian Abroad," by J. H. Hingston, the re-publication of a series of letters written to the Melbourne *Argus.*

Australia and New Zealand are on another great route of travel, and wintering there, the tourist may, at the close of the hurricane season—February and March—make a loop through that lazy, lovely, tropical realm, the South Sea, visit Samoa, Tahiti and Fiji, and from Levuka take ship back to Hong Kong. Steamers run frequently to the Philippines, and beside the great tobacco plantations of the islands and the factories, there is to be seen every evening on the Maidan, at Manilla, a parade of carriages and a show of wealth and luxurious living equal to that of any European capital. The Manilla Lottery is patronized throughout the Far East.

The grand route, however, is on to India, and the luxurious steamers give rest for a day at Singapore, that equatorial centre of the Eastern universe, where all the ways of commerce cross, and people of all nations, bound for all the remote corners of the globe, meet at the one famous hotel for their curries and cooling drinks.

At Colombo the tourist rests again for a day and tranships, or taking train for Kandy, climbs to the heights, sees Adam's Peak, Buddha's tooth, tea plantations, cinchona groves and coffee estates, and everywhere may buy the delusive sapphire and cat's-eye, manufactured perhaps at Birmingham for the globe-trotter trade.

From Ceylon the thorough-going tourist will go to Madras and work his way northward to Calcutta. December, January and February are the months for Indian travel. In the winter season, unfortunately, the hill stations are all but deserted, and nothing of Rudyard Kipling's Simla can be found in that place of barred and boarded houses; but the Himalayas show all their glory from the region about Darjheeli. As the viceroy moves his court from one ancient capital to another in the winter, staying a month at a time in each place, the visitor is sure of sometime happening upon all the pageantry and splendor he has imagined for the East.

From Bombay a ship conveys him further on the round, and once past the Red Sea, the real East is left—for Suez and the Levant are almost Europe to dwellers in Cathay—and then the Far East seems indeed a dream. _

JAPANESE WORDS AND PHRASES.

A few words and useful phrases in common Japanese speech may be easily learned, and will assist the tourist in dealing with the few shopkeepers, servants and coolies who do not understand a little English. A full command of Japanese, with a fluency in the polite forms of the court language, requires many years to acquire ; but with even a limited vocabulary the stranger has a greater range and independence.

All vowels have the continental sounds.

A is pronounced like *a* in father.

E is pronounced like *e* in prey or *a* in fate.

I is pronounced like *i* in machine or the English *e*.

O is pronounced like *o* in no.

U is pronounced like *oo* in moon.

AI has the sound of *i* in isle.

AU has the sound of *ow* in how.

SH has the sound of *sh* in shall.

HI is pronounced very nearly like *he* in sheaf

CH is pronounced soft, as in chance, chicken.

G has the the sound of *ng*, as Nagasaki (Nangasaki).

The consonants are pronounced as in English.

Each syllable is evenly accented, and only the *u* is sometimes elided, as Satsuma (Sats'ma), Dai Butsu (Dai Boots), etc.

The following conjugations, etc., are mostly taken from the small handbook of words and phrases first issued by Farsari & Co., Yokohama, but freely pirated since :

A short declination of the auxiliary verbs *suru*, to do, and *arimas*, to be, is here given, as many verbs can be formed from nouns in conjunctions with these as suffixes, and as all verbs can be declined by suffixing one of the auxiliaries ; e. g., Fatigue, *kutabire;* I am fatigued, *kutabiremashta; kiru*, to cut ; *kirimashta*, did cut ; *kirmasho*, will cut,

To Do—*Suru.*	To Have ; To Be—*Arimas.*
I do, *suru.*	I have ; I am, *arimas.*
I did, *shta.*	I have had ; I was, *arimashta.*
If I do, *shtareba.*	If I have, *arimashtareba.*
I will do, *shiyo*	I will have, *arimasho.*
I shall do, *suru de aru.*	I shall have, *aru de aru.*
Doing, *shte.*	Having ; being, *aru.*
I do not, *shinai.*	I have not ; I am not, *arimasen.*
I did not do, *shi-nakatta.*	I did not have ; I have not been, *arimasenanda.*
I will not do, *semai.*	I will not have ; I will not be, *arimasmai.*
Not doing, *sede; sedz.*	Not having ; not being, *naide.*
	Will you have? will you be? *arimaska.*
	Have you had ? *arimashtaka.*

63

There are no inflections to distinguish person or number in Japanese verbs, therefore *suru* will stand for "I do," as well as for "you do" or "he does."

Arimas is the compound word of *ari* and *masu*. *Ari* is the root of *aru*, to be; and *masu* is used with *aru* as a polite suffix. The word *gozarimas* so frequently heard is only the more polite form of *arimas*.

NOUNS, SENTENCES, ETC.

In Japanese NOUNS there are no inflections to distinguish gender, number and case, but the words *otoko*, *o* or *osu*, male, and *onna*, *me* or *mesu*, female, are used to distinguish gender; as, *otoko no uma*, horse; *onna no uma*, mare; *o ushi*, bull; *me ushi*, cow.

Osu and *mesu* are used when the noun is not mentioned, but understood.

Words with a *no* following are ADJECTIVES, with a *ni* following are ADVERBS.

The VERB comes at the end of the sentence and after the object governed by it; as *Inu wo* (the dog) *kaimashita* (I bought), I bought the dog. *To shimeru*, shut the door.

NUMBERS.

One, *ichi*.	Thirty, *san jiu*.
Two, *ni*.	Forty, *shi jiu* (and so on to ninety).
Three, *san*.	Hundred, *hyaku*.
Four, *shi*.	One hundred, *ippiaku*.
Five, *go*.	Two hundred, *ni hyaku*.
Six, *roku*.	Thousand, *sen*.
Seven, *shchi*.	One thousand, *issen*.
Eight, *hachi*.	Two thousand, *ni sen*.
Nine, *ku*.	Ten thousand, *man*.
Ten, *jiu*.	Hundred thousand, *jiu man*.
Eleven, *jiu ichi*.	Million, *hyaku man*.
Twelve, *jiu ni*.	Ten million, *sen man*.
Thirteen *jiu san* (and so on to nineteen).	Thirty-eight million, *San-sen hap-pyaku man*.
Twenty, *ni jiu*.	
Twenty-one, *ni jiu ichi*.	Billion, *cho*.
Once, *ichi do*.	Seven times, *shchi tabi*.
Twice, *ni do*.	Eight times, *hachi tabi*.
Three times, *san do*.	Nine times, *ku tabi*.
Four times, *yo tabi*.	Ten times, *jittabi*.
Five times, *go tabi*.	Double, *bai* or *nibai*.
Six times, *roku tabi*.	Triple, *sam bai*

MONTHS.

January, *sho gatsu*.	July, *shchi gatsu*.
February, *ni gatsu*.	August, *hachi gatsu*.
March, *san gatsu*.	September, *ku gatsu*.
April, *shi gatsu*.	October, *jiu gatsu*.
May, *go gatsu*.	November, *jiu ichi gatsu*.
June, *roku gatsu*.	December, *jiu ni gatsu*.

DAYS OF THE MONTH.

1st, *tsuitachi.*
2d, *futska.*
3d, *mikka.*
4th, *yokka.*
5th, *itska.*
6th, *muika.*
7th, *nanoka.*
8th, *yoka.*
9th, *kokonoka.*
10th, *toka.*
11th, *jiu ichi nichi.*
12th, *jiu ni nichi.*
13th, *jiu san nichi.*
14th, *jiu yokka.*
15th, *jiu go nichi.*
16th, *jiu roku nichi.*
17th, *jiu shchi nichi.*
18th, *jiu hachi nichi.*
19th, *jiu ku nichi.*
20th, *hatska.*
21st, *ni jiu ichi nichi.*
22d, *ni jiu ni nichi.*
23d, *ni jiu san nichi.*
24th, *ni jiu yokka.*
25th, *ni jiu go nichi.*
26th, *ni jiu roku nichi.*
27th, *ni jiu shchi nichi.*
28th, *ni jiu hachi nichi.*
29th, *ni jiu ku nichi.*
30th, *san jiu nichi* or *misoka.*
31st, *san jiu ichi nichi.*

DAYS OF THE WEEK.

Sunday, *nichi yobi.*
Monday, *gatsu* or *getsu yobi.*
Tuesday, *ka yobi.*
Wednesday, *sui yobi; nakadon.*
Thursday, *moku yobi.*
Friday, *kin yobi.*
Saturday, *do yobi; maidon.*

HOURS.

Hours are counted by prefixing the Chinese numerals to the Chinese word *ji*—"time," "hour"—thus :

ichi-ji, one o'clock.
ni-ji, two o'clock.
san-ji jip-pun, ten minutes past three.

yo-ji jiu-go-fun, fifteen minutes past four.
jiu-ji han, half-past ten.
jiu-ni-ji jiu-go-fun mae, fifteen minutes to twelve.

THE SEASONS.

Spring, *haru.*
Summer, *natsu.*
Autumn, *aki.*
Winter, *fuyu.*

DIVISIONS OF TIME.

Day, *hi.*
Morning *asa.*
Noon, *hiru; shogo.*
Evening, *yu; ban.*
Night, *yoru.*
Midnight, *yonaka.*
To-day, *konnichi.*
To-morrow, *myonichi.*
The day after to-morrow, *asatte; myogonichi.*

Yesterday, *sakujitsu.*
The day before yesterday, *ototoi; issakujitsu.*
An hour, *ichijikan.*
Half an hour, *hanjikan.*
A quarter of an hour, *ju go fun.*
Week, *shu.*
Month, *tsuki.*
One month, *hito-tsuki.*

65

THE HEAVENS.

Heavens, *ten*.
Sky, *sora*.
Sun, *taiyo; tento sama*.

Moon, *tski*.
Star, *hoshi*.

TRAVELING.

Passport, *ryokomenjo*.
Ticket, *kippu*.
Railway station, *suteishion*.
Post-office, *yubinkyoku*.
Telegraph office, *denshin kyoku*.
Inn, hotel, *yadoya*.
Carriage, *basha*.
Coachman, *gyosha betto*
Bath, *furo; yu*.
Bed, *nedoko*.
Room, *heya*.
Steamship, *jokisen* or *kisen*.
Steamship (side-wheel), *fune*.
Boatman, *sendo*.
Please return my passport,
    menjo o kaeshi nasai.
Railway train, *kisha; jokisha*.
Railway fare, *kishachin; chinsen*.
The rain comes in, *ame ga
    furikomu*.
Give me my bill, *kanjo okure*
Give me my receipt, *uketori,
    kudasai*.
What time does the train start?
    jokisha no deru wa nan ji?
Ticket, 1st class, *joto*.
Ticket, 2d class, *chiuto*.
Ticket, 3d class, *kato*.
Return ticket, *ofuku*.

What time is it? *nan doki des?*
I wish to go (name place), *e
    ikitai*.
Bring me some water, please,
    midzu wo motte kite okure.
Who is there? *dare da?*
Choose another word, please,
    hoka no kotoba o tskai nasai.
Is your master at home? *danna
    san o uchi de gozarimaska?*
What house is that? *nan no ie
    deska?*
Keep this till I come back, *kaeru
    made kore wo adzukatte kudasai*.
Post this letter, *kono tegamai wo
    yubin ni yatte kudasai*.
Are there any letters for me?
    tegami arimaska?
Send your messenger to me,
    anata no tskai wo yatte kudasai.
I wish to eat, I am hungry, *ta-
    betai*.
Please make me a fire, *hi wo
    tskero*.
Where are you going? *do chira
    oide nashaimas-ka?*
About how many miles? *nan ri
    hodo?*

IN THE JINRIKISHA.

Please tell me the road, *michi
    wo oshiete kudasai*.
Please get me a jinrikisha, *ku-
    ruma wo yonde kudasai*.
How much? *ikura?*
How much for one hour? *ichi ji
    kan ikura?*
Hurry up, go faster, *hayaku*.
Go slowly, *soro-soro*, or *shizuka
    ni iki*.
Stop, *mate* or *tomare*.
Stop a little, *sukoshi mate*.
Straight ahead, *massugu*.

Right, *migi*.
Left, *hidari*.
Take care, look out, *abunaiyo*.
Together, side by side, *issho ni*.
Enough, all right, *yoeoshi*.
Here and there, *achi kochi*.
This way, in this one, here, *ko-chira*.
That way, in that one, there, *achira*.
Where are you going? *doko maru?*
What? *nani?*
When? *itsu?*
Before, *saki*.
Behind, *ushiro*.

Have you? *arimaska?*
Have, I, *arimas.*
Have not, I, *arimasen.*
Know or understand, I, *waka-rimasu.*
Know or understand, I do not, *wakarimasen or shirimasen.*
Old, *furui.*
New, *atarashii.*
Cheap, *yasui.*
Cheap, very, *takusan yasui*
Dear, too much, *takai, amari takai* or *takusan takai.*
Crape, *chirimen.*
Crape (cotton), *chijimi.*
Brocade, *nishiki.*
Gown (clothing), *kimono.*
Coat, *haori.*
Sash, *obi.*
Thick, *atsui.*
Thin, *usui.*
Wide, *hiroi.*
Narrow, *semai.*
Long, *nagai.*
Short, *mijikai.*
Yard (measure), *shaku.* (Two and one-half *shaku* equal one English yard.)
Exchange, To, *tori kaeru.*
Black, *kroi.*
Blue, a wo, *sora-iro.*
Blue, dark, *asagi iro, kon.*
Blue, light, *mizu asagi.*
Green, *aoi; midori; moegi.*
Pink, *momo iro.*
Purple, *murasaki.*
Red, *akai.*
White, *shiroi.*
Yellow, *ki-iro.*
Fashion (mode), *hayari.*
Dirty, *kitanai.*
Best (No. 1,) the very best, *ichi ban uroshi.*

Large, *oki.*
Can or will do, I, *dekimas.*
Cannot or will not do, I, *dekimasen.*
It is impossible, *dekinai.*
Gold, *kin.*
Silver, *gin.*
Paper money, *satsu.*
Small, *chisai.*
Scissors, *hasami.*
Address it to, *shokai to na-ate wo kakinasai.*
I will take this also, *kore mo mochimasho.*
Let me see something better, *moto ii mono wo o mise nasai.*
Bring me samples of all you have, *arudake no mono mihon motte kite kudasai.*
I shall buy this, *kore wo kaimas.*
Let me know when it is ready, *shtaku shtareha shirase nasai.*
Please make it cheaper, *motto omake nasai.*
I want it of a lighter color, *moto usui iro ga hoshii.*
Give me one a good deal darker, *moto kroi iro kudasai.*
What is this made of? *kore wa nan de dekite orimas?*
How many? *ikutsu?*
Have you any more? *motto aru ka?*
Send this package to——, *kono tsutsumi* (name of place), *e yatte okure.*
I would like to see it, please, *misete okure.*
Less, *sukunai.*
The same thing, another like this, *onaji koto.*
Bad, *warui.*
Pretty, *kirei.*
I will come again, *mata kimasu.*

BEVERAGES, EATABLES, ETC.

Apple, *ringo.*
Beef, *ushi.*
Beer, *bir.*

Boil, To, *niru.*
Bread, *pan.*
Broil, To, *yakeru.*

BEVERAGES, EATABLES, ETC.—CONTINUED.

Butter, *gyuraku* (usually *batta*)
Cabbage, *botan na; kabiji.*
Cakes, *kashi.*
Carrot, *ninjin.*
Cherry, *sakura no mi.*
Chicken, *niwatori.*
Clams, *hamaguri.*
Claret, *budo sake.*
Codfish, *tara.*
Coffee, *kohi.*
Crab, *kani.*
Crayfish, *ise ebi.*
Cucumber, *kyuri.*
Eels, *unagi.*
Eggs, *tamago.*
Eggs, soft boiled, *tamago no han-jiku.*
Eggs, hard boiled, *tamago no ni-nuki.*
Figs, *ichijiku.*
Fish, *sakana.*
Flour, *udon no ko.*
Food, *tabemono.*
Fowl, *tori.*
Fruits, *kudamono; mizugashi.*
Grapes, *budo.*
Goose, *gacho.*
Hare, *usagi.*
Herring, *nishin.*
Lamb, *ko hitsuji no niku.*
Lemon, *yuzu.*
Mackerel, *saba.*
Meat, *niku.*
Melon, *uri.*
  Muskmelon, *makuwa uri.*
  Watermelon, *suika.*
Milk, *ushi no chichi.*
Mullet, *bora.*
Mustard, *karashi.*
Mutton, *hitsuji no niku.*
Oil, *abura.*
Omelet, *tamago yaki.*
Orange, *mikan.*

Oysters, *kaki.*
Pea, *endo mame.*
Peach, *momo.*
Pear, *nashi.*
Pepper, *kosho.*
Pheasant, *kiji.*
Pickles, *tskemono.*
Pigeon, *hato*
Plum, *ume.*
Pork, *buta.*
Potato, Irish, *jaga imo.*
Potato, sweet, *satsuma imo.*
Quail, *udzura.*
Rabbit, *usagi.*
Rice, *meshi; gozen.*
Roast, To, *yaku.*
Salad, *chisa.*
Salmon, *shake.*
Salt, *shiwo.*
Sardines, *iwashi.*
Shrimps, *yaku ebi.*
Snipe, *shigi.*
Soup, *tsuyu; o sui mono.*
Spinach, *horenso.*
Soy, *shoyu.*
Strawberries, *ichigo.*
Sugar, *sato.*
Tea, *o'cha.*
Tomato, *aka nasu.*
Trout, *yamome.*
Turkey, *shichimencho.*
Turnip, *kabu.*
Vegetables, *yasai.*
Vinegar, *su.*
Water, *midzu.*
Water, drinking, *nomi midzu.*
Water, hot, *yu.*
Whitebait, *shirago.*
Wine, *budoshu.*
Wine of the country, *sake.*

(For beer, brandy, whiskey, etc., the word "*sake*" is added to the English name.

FEATURES OF A COUNTRY.

Bay, *iri umi.*
Beach, *hama; umi-bata.*
Bridge, *hashi; bashi.*

Cape, *misaki.*
Capital, *miyako.*
Cascade, *taki.*

Cave, *hora ana.*
City, *machi; tokai.*
East, *higashi.*
Forest, *hayashi; mori.*
Gulf, *iri umi.*
Hill, *koyama.*
Harbor, *minato.*
Island, *shima; jima.*
Lake, *kosui; ike.*
Mountain, *yama.*
North, *kita.*

Peninsula, *eda shima.*
River, *kawa; gawa.*
Sea, *umi.*
South, *minami.*
Spring, *izumi; waki midzu.*
Street, *machi; tori.*
Tide, *shiwo.*
Town, *machi.*
Valley, *tani.*
Village, *mura.*
West, *nishi.*

OCCUPATIONS.

Officer, *yakunin.*
Teacher, *sensei.*
Captain, *sencho.*
Mate, *untenshi.*
Engineer, *kikanshi.*
Sailor, *suifu.*
Student, *shosei.*
Translator, *honyakusha.*
Interpreter, *tsuben.*
Farmer, *hyakusho.*
Manufacturer, *seizonin.*
Artist, *ekaki.*

Doctor, *isha.*
Surgeon, *geka isha.*
Photographer, *shashinshi.*
Dealer in foreign articles, *to-butsuya.*
Book-seller, *honya.*
Porcelain merchant, *setomonoya.*
Lacquer merchant, *shikkiya.*
Cook, *ryorinin.*
House boy, *kodzukai.*
Coolie, *ninsoku.*
Jinrikisha man *jinriki-hiki.*

GENERAL.

I am cold, *samui gozaimas.*
I will come again, *mata mairimas.*
As soon as possible, *narutake kayaku.*
What is your name? *o namae wa nan to moshimas?* (polite form); *na wa nanda?* (common form).
Will you come and have a drink? *kite ippai yarimasen ka?*
Foreign doctor, *seiyo no isha.*

I beg pardon, *gomen nasai.*
Yes, *saiyo; hei.*
No, *iye.*
Come here, please, *oide nasai.*
Thank you, *arigato.*
Good-bye, *sayonaro.*
Good-day, *kon nichi wa.*
Good-evening, *kon ban wa.*
Good-morning, *ohayo.*
Soon, right away, *tadaimo.*
Please, *dozo.*
What is your address? *anata no tokoro wa doko des ka?*

PHRASES USED BY NATIVES.

Irasshaimashi, welcome.
Hei kashkomarimashta, all right.
Omachidosama, sorry to keep you waiting.
Gokigen yo gozaimas, hope you are well.

Oagari nasai or *oagan nasai,* please come in; also used when goods or drink are offered—please partake.
Oainiku sama, we have none (of the article required).

Gokuro sama, many thanks for your kind trouble.

Naru hodo, I see, I see.

Yukkuri, please make yourself at home.

Ippuku o agari nasai, please take a smoke.

Oitoma itashimasho, I will now take my leave.

Yoku nashaimasta, glad you have come.

Yoku yoroshiku dozo, please give my regards to.

Gomen nasai, beg your pardon.

Doshtu? what is the matter?

Kekko, very good ; splendid.

LOCAL ENGLISH.

Amah, nurse.

Boy, house servant.

Bund, street facing the sea.

Bungalow, a one-story house.

Chit, note, letter, promise to pay.

Compound, enclosure, dwelling-place.

Curios, old bronzes, lacquer-ware, etc.

Compradore, agent through whom purchases or sales are made.

Godown, warehouse.

Griffin, a new arrival in the East ; also, a pony racing for the the first time.

Hatoba, jetty, landing.

Hong, a place of business.

Pyjamas, a loose suit worn at night.

Sampan, a native boat.

Shroff, silver expert.

Tiffin, luncheon.

CLIMATE—JAPAN.

TOKIO OBSERVATORY, 35° 41′ N. L., 139° 46′ E. L. Height 69 Feet, 13 Years, 1876–1888.

(Inches and Fahrenheit Degrees.)

	Jan.	Feb.	March	April	May	June	July	Aug.	Sept.	Oct.	Nov.	Dec.	Year.
Mean Temperature	36.7	37.9	43.9	53.8	61.5	69.9	75.9	77.9	71.1	60.3	49.6	41.0	56.5
Mean Maxima	46.8	47.1	53.6	62.6	68.2	75.6	83.1	85.6	78.8	69.9	59.9	52.0	65.3
Mean Minima	28.0	29.8	34.3	44.6	53.1	63.1	69.6	70.9	64.9	52.7	41.0	31.8	48.5
Absolute Maximum Temperature	On 14th	On July, 1886,											
Absolute Minimum Temperature	On 13th	On January,											
Mean Rainfall	2.20	3.27	10.8	4.47	5.49	5.48	4.85	3.86	8.42	7.86	1.91		58.33
Number of Rainy Days	7.1	9.6	10.8	14.3	18.6	14.9	13.9		14.8	13.7	8.14	6.4	138.7
Days with Snow	2.6	3.5	1.5	0.1							0.1	0.7	8.5

The "number of rainy days" includes all days on which more than a millimetre of rain fell, also those on which any snow or hail fell. The "days with snow" are those on which snow fell, regardless of the question whether rain also did or did not fall. Few days are uninterruptedly snowy at Tokio, perhaps only two or three in the year.

TABLE OF DISTANCES.

(DIRECT.)

	Hong Kong	Amoy	Woosung (Shanghai)	Nagasaki	Kobe (via Inland Sea)	Yokohama	Vancouver
	280	553	448	384	346	4300	
	811	810	765	710			
	1067	1120	765				
	1367	1340	1030				
	1591						

	Miles.
Vancouver to Montreal	2906
Montreal to Quebec	172
Quebec to Liverpool	2660
Montreal to Boston	342
New York to San Francisco	3266
Montreal to Halifax	756
Halifax to Liverpool	2480
Montreal to New York	383
New York to Liverpool	3180
San Francisco to Yokohama	4750

BOOKS OF REFERENCE

—on—

JAPAN AND CHINA.

"Murray's Hand Book for Travelers in Japan"—by B. H. Chamberlain and W. G. Mason.

"The Mikado's Empire"
"Fairy World" } —by W. E. Griffis. New York: Harper & Brothers

"Japan—Travels and Researches"
"The Industrial Arts of Japan" } —by J. J. Rein. New York: A. C. Armstrong & Son.

"Japan—Its Art, Architecture and Art Manufactures"—by Dr. Christopher Dresser. London: Longmans, Green & Co.

"Japanese Homes"—by Prof. E. S. Morse. New York: Harper & Brothers.

"Pictorial Arts of Japan"—by Dr. W. Anderson. London.

"Japanese Art and Artists"—by M. B. Huish. London; Fine Arts Society.

"Artistic Japan"—by S. Bing. Paris & London: Sampson, Marston & Lowe.

"An Artist's Letters from Japan"—by John La Farge. A Series of Papers in *The Century Magazine*, 1890.

"Japan—Its History, Traditions and Religion"—by Sir Edward Reid. London: John Murray.

"Unbeaten Tracks in Japan"—by Miss Isabella Bird. London: John Murray.

"Young Japan"—by J. R. Black.

"Japan—The Land of the Morning"—by W. G. Dixon. Edinburgh: J. Gammel.

"The Soul of the Far East"
"Noto; An Unexplored Corner of Japan" } —by Percival Lowell. Boston: Ticknor & Co.

"Seas and Lands"
"Japonica" } —by Sir Edwin Arnold. New York: Chas. Scribner's Sons, 1891.

"The Real Japan"—by Henry Norman. New York: Charles Scribner's Sons.

"Mme. Chrysantheme.' Paris Callmann-Levy.
"Japonaiseries d'Automne.' Paris: Callmann-Levy. } —by Pierre Loti.
"Japanese Women," *Harper's Magazine*, Dec, 1890.

"Japanese Girls and Women"—by Alice Bacon. Boston: Houghton, Mifflin & Co., 1891.

"Jinrikisha Days in Japan"—by Eliza Ruhamah Scidmore. New York: Harper & Brothers, 1891.

"Things Japanese"—by Basil Hall Chamberlain, 1891.

"A Flying Trip Around the World"—by Elizabeth Bisland. New York: Harper & Brothers, 1891.

"The Flowers of Japan and the Art of Floral Arrangement"—by Josiah Conder. Yokohama: Kelly & Walsh, 1891.

"Japanese Architecture"—by Josiah Conder and J. McD. Gardiner. (In Press.)

"Landscape Gardening in Japan"—by Josiah Conder. (In Press.)

"Japan As We Saw It"—by Robert S. Gardiner. Boston, 1892.

"Corea—The Hermit Nation"—by W. E. Griffis. New York: Harper & Brothers.

"Choson—The Land of the Morning Calm"—by Percival Lowell. Boston: Houghton, Mifflin & Co.

"The Middle Kingdom"—by S. Wells Williams. New York: Charles Scribner's Sons.

"Travels in Northern China"—by Rev. N. Williamson.

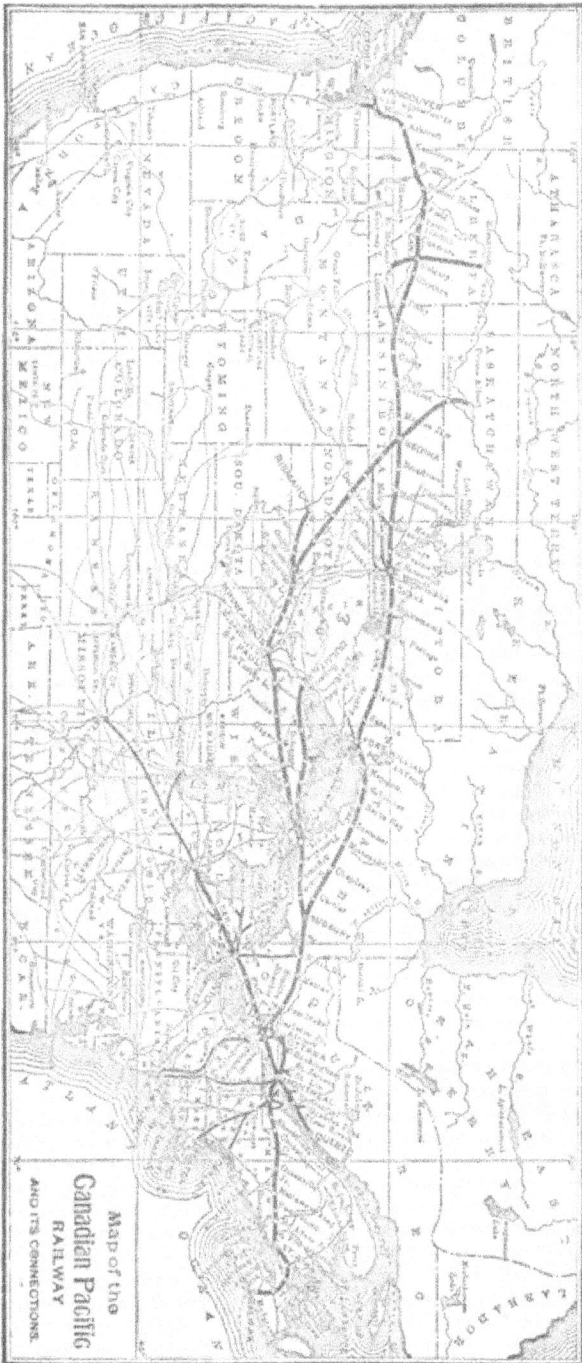

Map of the
Canadian Pacific
RAILWAY
AND ITS CONNECTIONS.

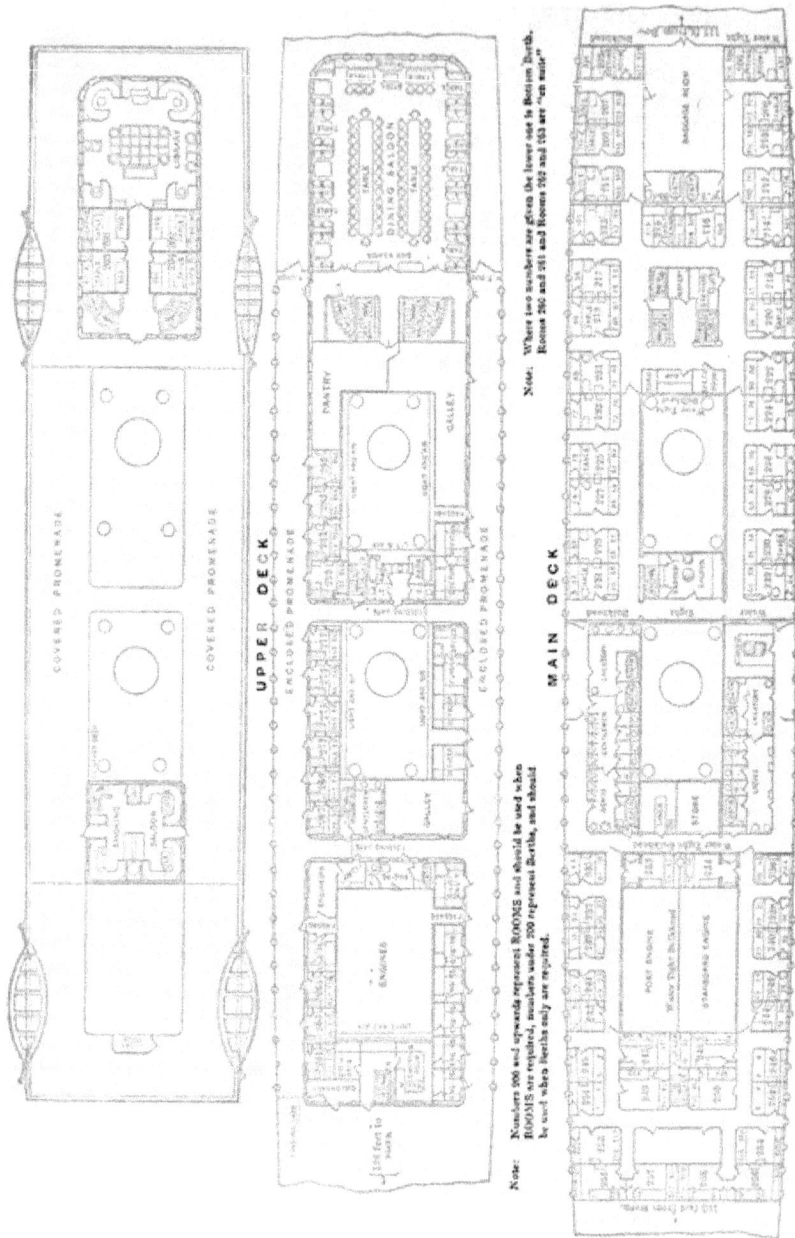

CABIN PLAN OF STEAMSHIPS "EMPRESS OF INDIA," "EMPRESS OF CHINA" AND "EMPRESS OF JAPAN."

COVERED PROMENADE

COVERED PROMENADE

UPPER DECK

ENCLOSED PROMENADE

ENCLOSED PROMENADE

DINING SALOON

PANTRY

GALLEY

ENGINES

MAIN DECK

PORT ENGINE

Water Tight Bulkhead

STARBOARD ENGINE

BAGGAGE ROOM

Note: Numbers 900 and upwards represent ROOMS and should be used when ROOMS are required, numbers under 900 represent Berths, and should be used where Berths only are required.

Note: Where two numbers are given the lower one is Bottom Berth. Rooms 260 and 261 and Rooms 262 and 263 are "en suite"

LOG RECORD.

Date.	Latitude.	Longitude.	Distance Run.	Remarks.

LOG RECORD.

STEAMSHIP.

Date.	Latitude.	Longitude.	Distance Run.	Remarks.

LIST OF PRINCIPAL AGENCIES

FROM WHOM DATES OF SAILING, TICKETS AND OTHER PARTICULARS
OF PASSAGE MAY BE OBTAINED.

———— ————

ADELAIDE...........AUS..Thos. Cook & Son.
AUCKLAND..........N. Z..L. D. Nathan & Co.
BALTIMORE.........MD..H. McMurtrie, Freight and Pass'r Agent.   - 203 E. German St.
BOMBAY............INDIA..Thomas Cook & Son,   -   -   -   -   13 Rampart Row.
BOSTON ....MASS.. { C. E. McPherson, Ass't Gen'l Pass'r Agent, 197 Washington St.
                           { H. J. Colvin, N. E. Pass'r Agent,   -   197 Washington St.
BRISBANE...........AUS..Thomas Cook & Son,   -   -   -   -   143 Queen St.
BROCKVILLE........ONT..G. E. McGlade, Ticket Agent,   -   -   -   143 Main St.
BUFFALO............N. Y..E. P. Allen, Freight and Pass'r Agent,   - 14 Exchange St.
CALCUTTA ....INDIA..Thomas Cook & Son,   -   -   -   - 11 Old Court House St.
CHICAGO .........ILL...J. Francis Lee, Dist. Freight and Pass'r Agent, 232 S. Clark St.
COLOMBO ....CEYLON..Thos. Cook & Son (E. B. Creasey).
DETROIT...........MICH..C. Sheehy, Dist. Pass'r Agent,   -   -   -   11 Fort St., W.
GLASGOW.....SCOTLAND..A. Baker, European Traffic Agent,   -   -   67 St. Vincent St.
HALIFAX ....N. S..C. S. Philps, Ticket Agent, -   -   -   -   126 Hollis St.
HAMILTON .........ONT..W. J. Grant,   -   -   -   -   -   8 St. James St. South.
HIOGO ....JAPAN..Frazar & Co.
HONG KONG ......CHINA..D. E. Brown, General Agent,   -   -   China, Japan, etc.
HONOLULU ....H. I..T. H. Davies & Co.
LIVERPOOL .........ENG..A. Baker, European Traffic Agent,   -   -   -   7 James St.
LONDON............ENG..   "   "   "   " 67 & 68 King William St., E. C.
LONDON............ONT..T. R. Parker, Ticket Agent,   -   -   - 161 Richmond St.
MALTA ....Turnbull, Jr. & Somerville, Correspondents.
MANCHESTER........ENG..A. Baker, European Traffic Agent,   -   -   105 Market St.
MONTREAL .........QUE..W. F. Egg, City Pass'r Agent,   -   -   129 St. James St.
MELBOURNE ....AUS..Thomas Cook & Son,   -   -   -   -   281 Collins St.
NEW YORK..........N. Y.. { F. V. Skinner, Gen'l East'n Agent, -   -   -   353 Broadway.
                           { Everett Frazar, China and Japan Freight Agent,   69 Wall St.
NIAGARA FALLS....N. Y..D. Isaacs,   -   -   -   -   -   -   Prospect House.
NIAGARA FALLS......ONT..George M. Colburn,   -   -   -   -   -   Clifton House
OTTAWA ...........ONT..J. E. Parker, City Pass'r Agent,   -   -   -   42 Sparks St.
PHILADELPHIA........PA..H. McMurtrie, Freight and Pass'r Agent, corner Third and
                           Chestnut Sts.
PORTLAND .........ME..G. H. Thompson,   -   -   -   -   Maine Central Rd. Station.
PORTLAND .........ORE..W. S. Hineline, Passenger Agent,   -   -   -   146 First St.
PT. TOWNSEND ....WASH..James Jones,   -   -   -   -   -   90 Taylor St.
QUEBEC ....QUE..George Duncan, Freight and Pass'r Agent,   - St. Louis Hotel.
RANGOON........BURMAH..Thomas Cook & Son,   -   -   -   -   Merchant St.
SHERBROOKE .......QUE..E. H. Crean, Ticket Agent, -   -   -   -   6 Commercial St.
ST. JOHN...........N. B..C. E. McPherson, Ass't Gen'l Pass'r Agent.
ST. PAUL ..........MINN..H. Brown,   -   -   -   -   -   -   183 East Third St.
SAN FRANCISCO......CAL..M. M. Stern, Dist. Freight and Pass'r Agent, Chronicle Building.
SAULT STE. MARIE, MICH..T. R. Harvey,   -   -   -   -   -   S. S. Wharf.
SEATTLE ..........WASH..E. W. MacGinnis,   -   -   "Starr-Boyd Building," Front St.
SHANGHAI ....CHINA..Jardine, Matheson & Co.
SYDNEY ....AUS.. { Huddart, Parker & Co.
                          { Thos. Cook & Son.
TACOMA...........WASH..W. R. Thompson, Freight and Pass'r Agent -   911 Pacific Av.
TORONTO ...........ONT..W. R. Callaway, Dist. Pass'r Agent,   -   -   1 King St. East.
VANCOUVER ....B. C.. { G. McL. Brown, Dist. Passenger Agent.
                           { James Sclater, Ticket Agent.
VICTORIA...........B. C..Allan Cameron, Freight and Pass'r Agent,   - Government St.
WINNIPEG..........MAN.. { Robt. Kerr, Gen'l Freight and Pass'r Agent, - W. & P. Divs.
                           { W. M. McLeod, City Ticket Agent,   -   -   - 471 Main St.
YOKOHAMA ......JAPAN..Frazar & Co.,   -   -   -   -   -   Agents for Japan.

——OR TO——

C. E. E. USSHER,   D. McNICOLL,
Ass't General Passenger Agent,   General Passenger Agent,

MONTREAL, QUE.

JULY							AUGUST							SEPTEMBER						
S	M	T	W	T	F	S	S	M	T	W	T	F	S	S	M	T	W	T	F	S
						1			1	2	3	4	5						1	2
2	3	4	5	6	7	8	6	7	8	9	10	11	12	3	4	5	6	7	8	9
9	10	11	12	13	14	15	13	14	15	16	17	18	19	10	11	12	13	14	15	16
16	17	18	19	20	21	22	20	21	22	23	24	25	26	17	18	19	20	21	22	23
23	24	25	26	27	28	29	27	28	29	30	31			24	25	26	27	28	29	30
30	31																			

1893

OCTOBER							NOVEMBER							DECEMBER						
S	M	T	W	T	F	S	S	M	T	W	T	F	S	S	M	T	W	T	F	S
1	2	3	4	5	6	7				1	2	3	4						1	2
8	9	10	11	12	13	14	5	6	7	8	9	10	11	3	4	5	6	7	8	9
15	16	17	18	19	20	21	12	13	14	15	16	17	18	10	11	12	13	14	15	16
22	23	24	25	26	27	28	19	20	21	22	23	24	25	17	18	19	20	21	22	23
29	30	31					26	27	28	29	30			24	25	26	27	28	29	30
														31						

JANUARY							FEBRUARY							MARCH						
S	M	T	W	T	F	S	S	M	T	W	T	F	S	S	M	T	W	T	F	S
	1	2	3	4	5	6					1	2	3					1	2	3
7	8	9	10	11	12	13	4	5	6	7	8	9	10	4	5	6	7	8	9	10
14	15	16	17	18	19	20	11	12	13	14	15	16	17	11	12	13	14	15	16	17
21	22	23	24	25	26	27	18	19	20	21	22	23	24	18	19	20	21	22	23	24
28	29	30	31				25	26	27	28				25	26	27	28	29	30	31

APRIL							MAY							JUNE						
S	M	T	W	T	F	S	S	M	T	W	T	F	S	S	M	T	W	T	F	S
1	2	3	4	5	6	7			1	2	3	4	5						1	2
8	9	10	11	12	13	14	6	7	8	9	10	11	12	3	4	5	6	7	8	9
15	16	17	18	19	20	21	13	14	15	16	17	18	19	10	11	12	13	14	15	16
22	23	24	25	26	27	28	20	21	22	23	24	25	26	17	18	19	20	21	22	23
29	30						27	28	29	30	31			24	25	26	27	28	29	30

1894

JULY							AUGUST							SEPTEMBER						
S	M	T	W	T	F	S	S	M	T	W	T	F	S	S	M	T	W	T	F	S
1	2	3	4	5	6	7				1	2	3	4							1
8	9	10	11	12	13	14	5	6	7	8	9	10	11	2	3	4	5	6	7	8
15	16	17	18	19	20	21	12	13	14	15	16	17	18	9	10	11	12	13	14	15
22	23	24	25	26	27	28	19	20	21	22	23	24	25	16	17	18	19	20	21	22
29	30	31					26	27	28	29	30	31		23	24	25	26	27	28	29
														30						

OCTOBER							NOVEMBER							DECEMBER						
S	M	T	W	T	F	S	S	M	T	W	T	F	S	S	M	T	W	T	F	S
	1	2	3	4	5	6					1	2	3							1
7	8	9	10	11	12	13	4	5	6	7	8	9	10	2	3	4	5	6	7	8
14	15	16	17	18	19	20	11	12	13	14	15	16	17	9	10	11	12	13	14	15
21	22	23	24	25	26	27	18	19	20	21	22	23	24	16	17	18	19	20	21	22
28	29	30	31				25	26	27	28	29	30		23	24	25	26	27	28	29
														30	31					

MAP
OF THE
Canadian Pacific Railway Co.'s
STEAMSHIP ROUTE.
CENTRAL AND SOUTHERN JAPAN.

Engraved by SMITH, GARDNER & Co. "Offd 42 & 52 Rd."

Scale of English Miles

———— Open Lines of Railway
———— Lines under construction
———— C. P. R. Steamer Line

YOKOHAMA

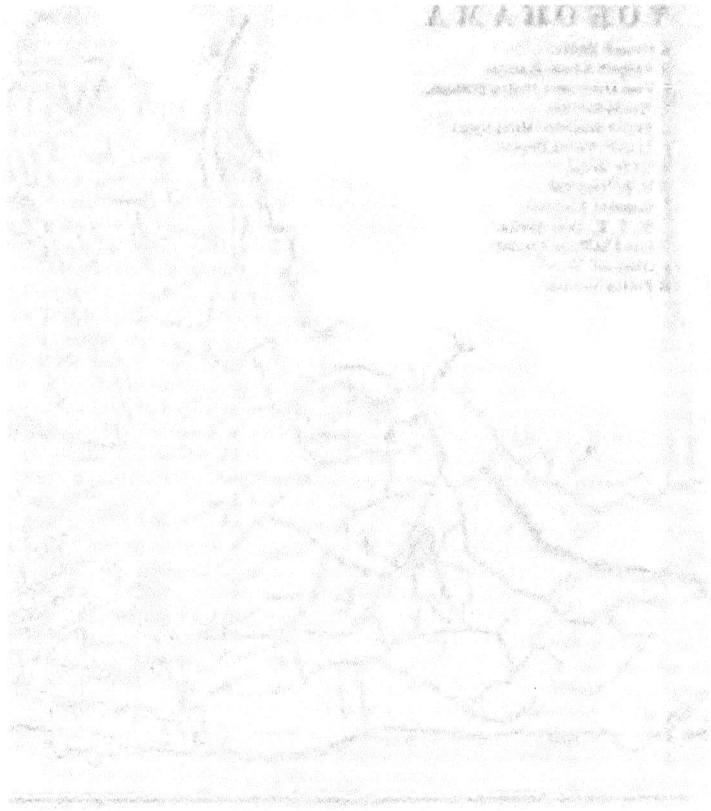

www.ingramcontent.com/pod-product-compliance
Lightning Source LLC
Chambersburg PA
CBHW020328090426
42735CB00009B/1451